Praise for the *Intelligent Patient Guide* series

*The guide to breast cancer walks you through each step of
your diagnosis, treatment and prognosis...with explanations
that are easily understood. It brought everything together,
making it so clear.*
— J. McIntosh, Patient

*A guide not only to breast cancer but to breast health
and early detection of disease, the* Intelligent Patient Guide
to Breast Cancer *should be part of* every *woman's
personal library.*
— Cheryl Edwards MA
High School Teacher

*One of the best explanations of breast cancer risk I've seen
in print...dispells the 'panic' of the 'I in 9' statistics...
It's lovely to see in print many of the teachings we use
on a daily basis.*
— Barbara Warren RN
Director of Nursing,
Manitoba Cancer Treatment and Research Foundation

*As a patient advocate and breast cancer survivor, I lend
and use my copy of the* Intelligent Patient Guide *often.
The book helps equip patients to better understand the need
to take charge in the design of their own survival.*
— B. Cameron

*It was so informative. I felt so secure knowing what was
going to happen with every step.*
— D. Powell, Patient

Intelligent Patient Guide To

Breast Cancer

Intelligent Patient Guide To

Breast Cancer

All you need to know to take
an active part in your treatment

Ivo Olivotto MD
Karen Gelmon MD
Urve Kuusk MD

edited by
Carol Glegg BSc

Intelligent Patient
GUIDE

Vancouver, 1996

While the authors have made every effort to ensure that the material contained herein is accurate at time of publication, new discoveries or changes in treatment practices may ultimately invalidate some of the information presented here.

Intelligent Patient Guide Ltd.
517-750 West Broadway
Vancouver, British Columbia V5Z 1H4
Canada
http://www.ipguide.com

Copyright © 1996 by Intelligent Patient Guide Ltd.

Canadian Cataloguing in Publication Data
Olivotto, Ivo, 1956-
    The Intelligent Patient Guide to Breast Cancer

    (Intelligent Patient Guide)
    Includes bibliographical references and index.
    ISBN 0-9696125-2-4

    1. Breast—Cancer—Popular works. I. Gelmon, Karen, 1953-
    II. Kuusk, Urve, 1950 - III. Title. IV. Series.
RC280.B8044 1995   616.99'449   C94-910968-1

Typeset in Sabon by Cait Beattie, Montreal
Cover design by Chris Dahl, Art & Design, West Vancouver
Printed in Canada

Distributed by
Gordon Soules Book Publishers Ltd.
1354-B Marine Drive, West Vancouver, BC
Canada V7T 1B5
620-1916 Pike Place, Seattle, WA 98101, US
(604) 922 6588 Fax: (604) 688 5442
E-mail: books@gordon.soules.com

This book is dedicated to the thousands of women who have lived and are living with breast cancer and who, through their stories and their strength, have taught us so much.

Part of the proceeds from the sale of this book will go towards programs of Breast Cancer information, support and research.

Authors (from left to right): Urve Kuusk MD,
Ivo Olivotto MD, and Karen Gelmon MD

Authors

Ivo Olivotto, MD, FRCPC
Chair, Breast Tumor Group,
British Columbia Cancer Agency;
Clinical Associate Professor,
Division of Radiation Oncology,
University of British Columbia

Karen Gelmon, MD, FRCPC
Head, Section of Investigational New Drugs,
British Columbia Cancer Agency;
Clinical Associate Professor,
Division of Medical Oncology,
University of British Columbia

Urve Kuusk, MD, FRCSC
Clinical Assistant Professor,
Division of General Surgery,
University of British Columbia

Editor
Carol Glegg, BSc

Illustrator
Jane Rowlands, BSc (Art as Applied to Medicine)

Coordinator
Maria Issa, PhD

Contributing Authors
Carolyn Baker, RN
Clinical Nurse Specialist,
Vancouver Hospital & Health Sciences Centre

Judith Caldwell
President, Canadian Breast Cancer Foundation,
British Columbia Chapter

Shirley Hobenshield, RDN
Registered Dietitian-Nutritionist,
British Columbia Cancer Agency

Michael E. Pezim, MD, FRCSC, FACS
Associate Professor, Department of Surgery,
University of British Columbia;
Consultant Surgeon, British Columbia Cancer Agency

Lis Smith, CCH
Clinical Hypnotherapist,
Division of Patient and Family Counselling,
British Columbia Cancer Agency

Richard Warren, MD, FRCSC
Head, Division of Plastic Surgery,
University of British Columbia

Cynthia Webster, BSR
Registered Physical Therapist,
Quest Physiotherapy,
Vancouver

Why read this book?

AFTER YOUR DOCTOR SAYS the words 'breast cancer' you may be in a state of shock. Despite this, you will be expected to make a series of major decisions, often in a hurry. 'Should I have a mastectomy? Should I have radiation? Chemotherapy? Tamoxifen?' The choices seem so complicated. Women often end up wondering, 'Should I just leave the decisions up to my doctors and do whatever they suggest?'

We believe not. Time and again we have seen that the patient who takes an active part in making the decisions that affect the course of her treatment is better able to cope than the patient who relegates all control to her doctors. While we are not advocating that you make choices independently of the recommendations of your doctor, we encourage you to become one of the decision-makers. We have written this book with the purpose of providing you with the information you will need to fulfill this role.

It is important to note that the statistics we have quoted about risks and prognosis refer to general or 'average' situations. Special additional circumstances may modify your individual risk and need to be discussed with your doctor.

We hope this book can help you move through the fear, to a place of hope and strength and the promise of life ahead — in spite of breast cancer.

Ivo Olivotto MD
Karen Gelmon MD
Urve Kuusk MD

Table of Contents

CONTINUED

PART ONE | **Breast cancer: What is it and how is it detected?**

SECTION ONE

The Normal Breast

CHAPTER ONE

Breast anatomy and function

THE BREAST IS MUCH MORE EXTENSIVE than most people realize. (Figure 1). Breast tissue can be found as high as the collar bone (clavicle), and extends from almost the middle of the chest over the breast bone (sternum) to the armpit (axilla).

What's in the breast?

The breast is made up of milk glands, tubes (ducts) that carry the milk to the nipple, and fat.

The milk is produced in hundreds of thousands of tiny glands within the breast called lobules (Figure 2). The lobules are drained by small ducts that collect the milk into larger glands that look like tiny bunches of grapes. From here, big ducts carry the milk to the nipple. The nipple surface contains about 20 duct openings, each draining a different part of the breast. All the milk glands are cushioned by fat. The normal 'lumps' that you feel in your breast every day are a combination of the milk glands, fat, and other fibrous tissues.

The proportion of milk glands, ducts and fat in the breast changes as you get older. During puberty, and as the breast develops it consists mainly of ducts. However, in a 20-year-old

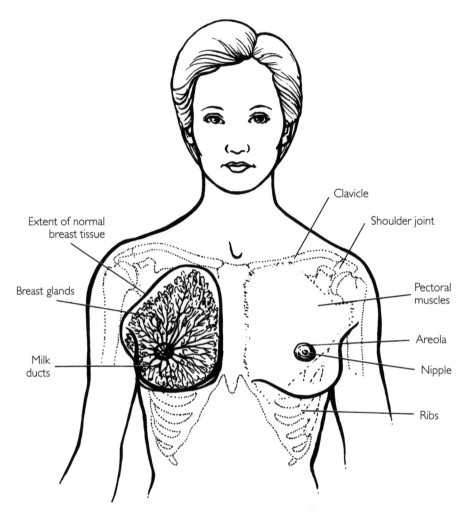

Clavicle

Shoulder joint

Extent of normal
breast tissue

Breast glands

Pectoral
muscles

Areola

Milk
ducts

Nipple

Ribs

Figure 1: Extent of normal breast tissue and important underlying structures.

woman most of the breast is made up of milk glands. During pregnancy and breastfeeding (lactation) the glandular content of the breast increases dramatically as the breast becomes prepared to produce milk.

The fat content increases as you age, especially after menopause. In an elderly woman almost all of the breast is fatty tissue. However, hormones taken after menopause maintain the glandular tissue and delay the normal fatty replacement.

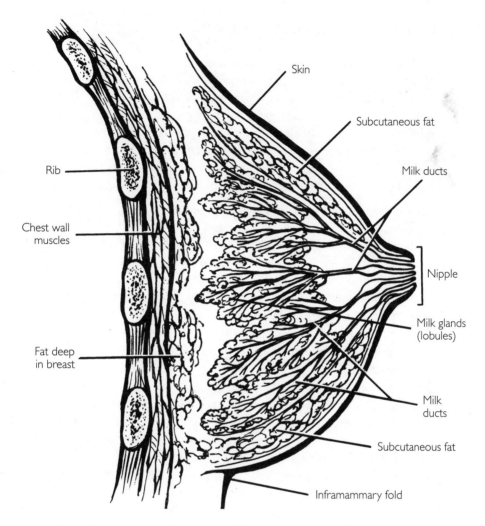

Figure 2: A cross-sectional view of the breast showing the internal appearance of the breast and its relationship to the chest wall.

Ligaments help hold the breast in place

Throughout the breast there are many supporting ligaments, like very thick, strong elastic bands, that connect onto the breast bone or muscles under the breast. With age, these ligaments tend to stretch and the normal breast begins to sag.

7

Muscles around the breast

A large, fan-shaped muscle lies beneath most of the breast. This is the *pectoralis major* muscle which is responsible for some of the movements of the shoulder and arm. You can feel this muscle as a firm ridge extending from the outside edge of the breast toward the armpit if you tense your arm and 'push in' with your hand on your hip. The *pectoralis minor* muscle is smaller and is not readily felt.

Lymph nodes: where infection fighting occurs

The purpose of the lymphatic system is to fight off infections in the body. Like blood vessels, there are tiny lymph vessels in every organ and tissue of the body. Fluid which normally leaks out of blood vessels to bathe the body tissues is collected by the lymph vessels and carried to groups of lymph nodes located at various places in the body. In the lymph nodes infections are 'filtered out' and destroyed. The 'treated' fluid then enters the blood stream.

Figure 3 shows the location of the main groups of lymph nodes that drain the breast. They are just above the armpit, above the collarbone, and along the sternum (the internal mammary lymph nodes). You have between 30 and 50 lymph nodes in the armpit.

Lymph nodes are of particular importance in breast cancer. Breast cancer cells sometimes enter the lymphatic vessels that drain the breast and may be carried to the lymph nodes where they settle and grow. The single most important factor in determining the future behavior of a breast cancer is if any cancer cells are found to be living and growing within the lymph nodes at the time of diagnosis (see Chapter 13).

Sensation and the nerves around the breast

Many nerves pass through the breast to the skin and to the nipple. In addition, the intercostal-brachial nerves come from the area between the ribs, through the armpit (axilla) and reach

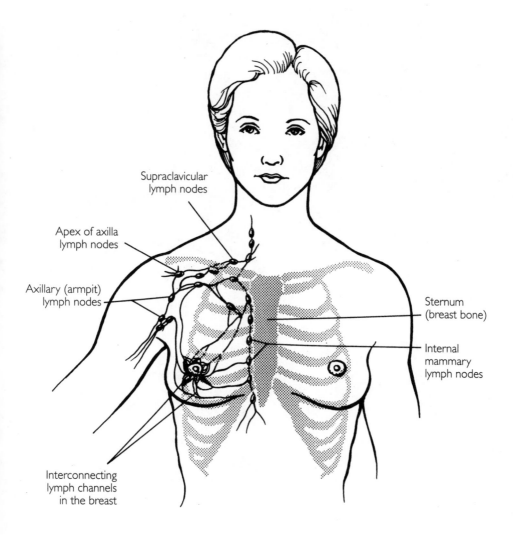

Supraclavicular
lymph nodes

Apex of axilla
lymph nodes

Axillary (armpit)
lymph nodes

Interconnecting
lymph channels
in the breast

Sternum
(breast bone)

Internal
mammary
lymph nodes

Figure 3: System of lymph nodes that drain the breast.

to the underside or back of the upper arm. These nerves are often stretched or cut during surgery in the armpit which leads to an unpleasant tingling, burning, numb or 'thick' sensation on the back or underside of the upper arm. This may fade partly or completely over several months after surgery, but if the nerves have been cut, the numbness is permanent.

What Is Breast Cancer?

Chapter Two

What is cancer?

To UNDERSTAND WHAT CANCER IS, it is important to first understand how the body's cells normally work.

How does the body grow and maintain itself?

The body is made up of tiny cells, for example, skin cells, muscle cells, heart cells, nerve cells and bone cells. When a baby grows the number of cells increases very quickly. A cell becomes a bit larger, then divides into two 'daughter' cells (Figure 4). After a period of time each of these cells divides again, and so on.

Figure 4: Normal cell division. A cell grows a bit larger and then divides into two cells.

Once a child grows to adulthood the size of the body no longer increases. However, our bodies go through a lot of wear and tear, both inside and outside. 'Upkeep' means that worn-out cells constantly need to be replaced, so cell division still takes place, but more slowly. An obvious 'outside' change is the tiny bits of dead skin flaking off as the skin constantly renews itself.

Although our bodies' cells continue to divide to replace worn-out cells, this happens in a very ordered, systematic way. The reason is that each cell carries genetic 'instructions' that regulate how fast the cell should divide and 'grow' and when the cell should die. A balance between cells growing and dying keeps our bodies functioning normally.

When cell growth goes out of control

Benign growths

Sometimes a cell starts to grow without regard for the normal balance between cell growth and death, and a small, harmless lump of cells will form. These harmless growths are referred to as 'benign.' A benign growth can occur in any part of the body, including the breast, skin or intestine.

Malignant growths

In other cases a cell may grow and divide with complete disregard for the needs and limitations of the body. They have the potential to grow into large masses or spread to other areas of the body. Cells that have this aggressive behavior are called 'malignant.' More commonly, a mass of such cells is called a 'cancer.' When clumps of these cells spread to other parts of the body they are termed 'metastases.' A cancer that continues to grow can eventually overwhelm and destroy the part of the body or particular organ where it is located.

Cancer cells also have the ability to stimulate the development of blood vessels to increase their own blood supply and enhance their growth. Sometimes, however, a cancer's wild growth rate backfires. The cancer may grow so rapidly that it can't get enough oxygen and nutrients from the blood vessels. When this happens a part of the cancer may suddenly die. This death of a group of cells within a cancer is known as 'necrosis.'

Cancer cells have the ability to spread

In addition to controlled growth, most normal cells remain in the area where they belong and don't spread to other parts of the body. Cancer cells disregard this principle and may spread through the body (metastasize) in several ways (Figure 5). These include direct invasion and destruction of the organ of origin, or spread through the lymphatic system and/or blood stream to distant organs such as the lungs, liver and bones.

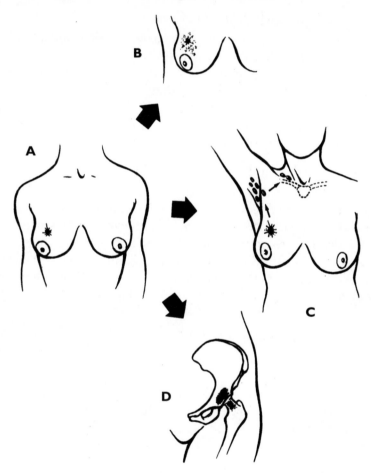

Figure 5: Mechanisms of spread of a breast cancer. A cancer (A) grows and spreads by direct local invasion (B) of the breast itself or (C) through the lymphatic system to lymph nodes or (D) through the blood stream to distant organs such as the bones, lungs, liver or brain.

When a cancer spreads it retains the properties of the original cancer. This means that a breast cancer that spreads to the bones is still a breast cancer. Under the microscope it looks different from a cancer that started in the bones, and it responds to treatment like a breast cancer, not a bone cancer.

The original cancer in the breast is called the 'primary' cancer. A cancer that has spread to another site is called a 'secondary' or 'metastatic' cancer.

Cancer cells can trick the immune system

The immune system consists of a group of cells called 'white blood cells,' specialized to recognize and destroy 'foreign' material in the body such as bacteria, viruses and unfamiliar or abnormal cells. Cancer cells somehow manage to slip through this detection system without triggering the immune system to start fighting, either at the primary cancer site, in the blood vessels, or at the site of distant spread.

Breast cancer does not develop overnight

It can take years of cells dividing before a normal cell becomes a cancerous cell. The cell first undergoes very small changes in which it becomes slightly abnormal or 'atypical' as seen under a microscope. It may also begin to divide, grow more quickly and accumulate in excessive numbers (hyperplasia). Then, over the years the cells continue to change, become more abnormal-looking and finally cancerous (Figure 6).

| Normal
milk
duct | Hyperplasia
(too many
cells) | Atypia
(cells becoming
abnormal) | In situ cancer
(cancer cells
inside the ducts) | Invasive cancer
(cells spread out
of the duct) |

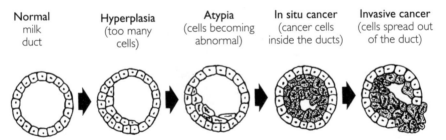

Figure 6: Breast cancer does not develop overnight. Gradually the cells become more abnormal-looking or atypical (see text). Eventually, the cells are recognized as being sufficiently abnormal to be called cancer cells that are initially inside the milk ducts (in situ cancer), and later become invasive breast cancer cells.

Initially the cancer cells are confined within the milk ducts (in situ cancers), but with time the cells develop the ability to invade out of the ducts and into the blood and lymphatic system (an invasive cancer).

Unfortunately, it is not possible to detect one or a few abnormal or cancer cells. At present, technology is only capable of detecting a small lump or mass of cancer cells that has already started to grow. By the time a cancer can be detected as a lump, it may have been growing slowly for anywhere from two to eight years.

CHAPTER THREE

How common is breast cancer?

BREAST CANCER IS THE MOST COMMON type of cancer in women. In 1994 there were over 16,300 new cases diagnosed and 5,400 deaths from breast cancer in Canada and approximately ten times that number in the USA. Breast cancer accounts for 4% of all deaths of women in North America each year and the loss of thousands of productive years of life.

'One in nine' is misleading

One often hears that 'one in ten' or 'one in nine' (lately even 'one in eight') women will get breast cancer. The trouble with these figures is that they are misleading because they don't tell the whole story. The figure 'one in nine,' for example, refers to the chance that a woman will develop breast cancer *if she lives to the age of 90*. A crucial point to realize, however, is that the risk of breast cancer increases with increasing age. Women over 70, for example, are at least four times more likely to get breast cancer than women who are under 40 years old. Not only that, but the majority of women die before the age of 90, so they don't reach the oldest age group where the high risk of breast cancer accumulates that pushes the overall lifetime risk up to 'one in nine.' For most women, therefore, the risk of getting breast cancer is much lower than one in nine.

Recent changes in the incidence of breast cancer

Since the early 1980s there has been a definite increase in the number of cases of breast cancer identified each year in North America. (The rate of detection of new cases is referred to as 'incidence'.) Much of this recent increase has been attributed to the increased use of screening mammography since the mid-1980s. This is because screening mammography can detect some cancers two to five years before they would reach the size where a lump can be felt by the woman or her doctor. However, once the entire population undergoes mammographic screening at least once, then this sudden 'wave' of earlier detected cancers will become the new standard, and the incidence rates should drop again. In other words, it's not that there are suddenly more cancers, but that a new method of detection is finding more cancers earlier than would otherwise have been the case with older methods.

You can estimate your own risk

Rather than considering a lifetime risk to age 90, a more useful question is: 'What is my risk, given my current age?'

Table 1 shows the average risk each year of developing breast cancer for typical North American women at specific ages.

Table I	Annual (not lifetime) risk of developing breast cancer
At age	Risk
30 years	I in 6,000 per year
40 years	I in 1,200 per year
50 years	I in 550 per year
60 years	I in 400 per year
70 years	I in 300 per year
80 years	I in 250 per year

Table 2	Chance of developing breast cancer by a given age
Age	Lifetime risk
25 years	less than 1 in 1,000
50 years	1 in 63
75 years	1 in 15
90 years	1 in 9

Table 2 shows not the annual risk, but the lifetime risk up to certain ages. Using Table 1, based on her current age, the 'average' woman can estimate her risk of developing breast cancer over the next year.

The risk over the next decade is 10 times the annual risk. For example, if you are 42, your annual risk is slightly higher than that of the 40-year-old listed in Table 1, say 1/1,000 per year. Over the next decade your risk would be 10 × 1/1,000 = 1/100 or approximately 1%. This risk is much easier to live with than one in nine. As you can see from Table 2, even a woman who is 75 years old does not yet have a 'one in nine' chance of developing breast cancer. More specific, individualized risk estimates can be determined by considering additional factors that are associated with a higher risk of developing breast cancer, and then multiplying the 'average' risk at a certain age by the risk factor. Chapter 4 discusses some of the causes of breast cancer and ranks them according to their importance.

CHAPTER FOUR

What causes breast cancer?

Why me?

'WHY DID I GET BREAST CANCER?' This is a question that doctors can almost never answer with any accuracy. However, it is not your 'fault' or 'punishment' for something you did or did not do. It is not something to be ashamed of.

There has been a lot of controversy over the years about the possible causes of breast cancer: diet, hormones, genetic make-up, or substances in the environment. Today we realize that probably there is no single factor that causes breast cancer, but that it is a combination of things, some more important than others.

What is a risk factor?

A 'risk factor' refers to something that increases your chances of getting a disease, in this case, breast cancer. A strong risk factor greatly increases the chances, while a weak risk factor just slightly increases your chances. For example, in the case of lung cancer, smoking is a very strong risk factor. In other words, someone who smokes is far more likely to get lung cancer than someone who doesn't.

With breast cancer there are several known risk factors, ranging from strong to weak (see Table 3).

A 'strong' risk factor is defined as something that increases the chance of getting breast cancer by more than four times (compared to someone without this risk factor). 'Moderate' means an increase of two to four times the risk, and 'weak' means less than two times the risk.

Strong risk factors

Increasing age is a strong risk factor for developing breast cancer. Women who are 50 years old have double the risk of women who are 40, and the risk doubles again by the age of 70 years (see Table 1, p. 19). For three-quarters of women who get breast cancer, getting older is the only identifiable risk factor. The remaining 25% of women with breast cancer have a combination of other risk factors.

Previous history of breast cancer

Most women who get one breast cancer do not get another. However, every year about one in every 200 women with a first breast cancer will develop another cancer in the opposite breast. Women with the lobular type of breast cancer (see Chapter 15) have a higher yearly chance, about one in every 100, of getting cancer in the opposite breast. Since there is no proven way to prevent these cancers other than by removing the entire opposite breast, it is important to keep the second breast under surveillance with regular self-examinations and examinations conducted by your physician, and an annual mammogram (breast x-ray).

Family history of breast cancer

A family history of breast cancer in a close relative such as your mother, sister, or daughter contributes to your risk. However, breast cancer in a more distant relative such as an aunt or grandmother has little or no impact on your risk. A history of breast cancer in a premenopausal close relative, breast cancer in more than one close relative, or cancer in both breasts of a close relative confers a four to six times higher risk of devel-

Table 3 **Risk factors associated with the development of breast cancer**		
Strong (Risk greater than 4× normal)	Moderate (Risk greater than 2-4× normal)	Weak (Risk greater than 1-2× normal)
Female sex

Advancing age

Previous cancer in one breast (especially lobular carcinoma)

Family history of breast cancer: premenopausal or in both breasts

Past breast biopsy showing severely abnormal cells and hyperplasia | Over 30 years old at birth of first child

Past breast biopsy: any sign of cell abnormality or hyperplasia

Postmenopausal obesity

Diet (possibly) | First menses before the age of 12 years

Menopause after the age of 54 years

Family history of breast cancer: older, postmenopausal

Prolonged hormone use (more than 15 years)

Moderate to heavy alcohol consumption

Ethnic origin |

oping breast cancer compared to a woman of the same age who does not have relatives with breast cancer.

There are rare families in which three or more generations have several relatives with breast cancer. In some of these families the disease may be passed on by a specific genetic mutation. For example, families with the BRCA1 gene inherit a tendency to develop both breast and ovarian cancer. Women who inherit such a mutation have a risk of developing breast cancer as high as 80% by the age of 50. Many of these families are characterized by breast cancer developing in young, premenopausal women, with the disease often appearing five to ten years earlier with each generation.

Moderate risk factors

Later pregnancy

A first child delivered before the age of 20 causes certain permanent hormonal changes and provides a modest protection against breast cancer. Delaying the first child until after the age of 30 or delivering no children increases the risk two to four times. Breastfeeding may decrease the chance of getting breast cancer by a small amount.

Previous breast biopsy showing abnormal cells or excessive accumulation of cells (hyperplasia)

As described in Chapter 1, a normal cell becomes a cancer cell through a series of changes in which the cells begin to divide and accumulate in excessive numbers (hyperplasia), become abnormal (atypical) and finally develop into cancer cells. If hyperplasia is seen in tissue removed during a breast biopsy, especially with atypical cells, the woman has a two to four times greater chance of developing breast cancer compared to a woman without these changes. If there is severe atypia and hyperplasia, especially in a woman who also has a family history of breast cancer, an eight-fold increased risk can be expected.

Weak risk factors

Generally, women who use oral contraceptives do not increase their risk of breast cancer. Some studies suggest that there is a modestly higher risk among women who, when they were young, took the older, high-dose estrogen type pill for many years (more than seven to ten years continuously). Modern oral contraceptive pills have a lower estrogen content, so that with 10 to 15 years of use they can be considered to cause no appreciable increase in the risk of developing breast cancer.

The onset of menstrual periods before the age of 12 years and cessation of menstruation after the age of 52 years weakly increase the risk of breast cancer.

Postmenopausal estrogen

The risk associated with postmenopausal estrogen use ('hormone replacement therapy') is more controversial. Overall, women who have at some point used estrogen alone (Premarin® and others) or estrogen in combination with progesterone (Provera® and others) do not have a higher chance of developing breast cancer as compared with women who have never used these medications. However, women who have taken post-menopausal hormones for longer than 15 years have an approximately 1.5-fold increased risk compared to the risk among non-users. This modestly higher breast cancer risk following long-term hormone use has to be considered in context with the potentially beneficial effects of these medications, including, among other things, a lower risk of bone fractures, fewer heart attacks and strokes, and relief of hot flashes, vaginal dryness and mood swings which may accompany menopause.

Diet and body weight

There has been extensive research into the role of diet in the formation of breast cancer. Some authorities believe that up to 30% of breast cancers may be attributable to dietary influences.

Studies of populations which move from an area associated with low breast cancer risk (e.g. Japan) to an area of high risk (e.g. North America) show that within one to two generations the migrant population adopts the risk level of the new country. This is thought to be due to changes of diet and life style which the children and grandchildren of the immigrants adopt.

It is not clear which dietary factors are important. The principal culprit thought to be associated with breast cancer is dietary fat, but this is still not proven. Furthermore, it is not known which type of dietary fat may be the culprit: saturated or unsaturated, fat of vegetable or animal origin, or whether the effect is simply related to overeating.

Moderate to heavy alcohol consumption (more than three drinks or six glasses of wine per week) has been associated with a weak increase in the risk of developing breast cancer. However, it remains reasonable to have an occasional drink or glass of wine.

Obesity during the postmenopausal years has been associated with a small increase in breast cancer risk. Interestingly, being markedly underweight in the premenopausal years also increases the risk, while premenopausal obesity does not.

Environmental factors

Radiation from x-rays is a common concern. Even at low doses, the use of x-rays in younger women (less than 20 years old) has been associated with an increased risk of breast cancer. However, the usual dose of radiation from a mammogram (x-ray of the breast) is very small, and most authorities estimate that the risk of inducing a breast cancer is extremely remote, less than one case in one to two million, compared to the beneficial effects of being able to identify a cancer and begin early, effective treatment. Also, routine mammograms tend to be used in women older than 40 (see Chapter 6) who are more resistant to the effects of radiation than younger women.

Chemical carcinogens are everywhere in our environment, but no specific chemical or substance has been identified as specifically causing a greater number of breast cancers. Although recently there has been concern about organochlorines found in pesticides, so far there is no association confirmed between the use of pesticides and incidence of breast cancer.

Smoking does not appear to either increase or decrease the risk of developing breast cancer.

Race: little if any effect on risk

Historically, in the USA, blacks have had a lower incidence of breast cancer than whites, but unfortunately the survival rate for blacks is lower than the survival rate for whites. This has been attributed to differences in access to medical care. In Canada, the age-adjusted risk among aboriginal women seems to be lower than that among caucasians.

Since ethnic groups who migrate to North America from areas of low risk (e.g. Japan and Southeast Asia) adopt the higher risk of the 'average' woman in North America within one to two generations, this strongly suggests that the influences of race, ethnic background and genetics have little, if any role compared to diet, life style or other environmental factors.

CHAPTER FIVE

Prevention – Is it possible?

Risk factors we cannot change

IT IS FRUSTRATING that the major known risk factors for developing breast cancer cannot be changed, such as female sex, advancing age, family or previous personal history of breast cancer and the age at which menstrual periods begin (see Chapter 4). Getting pregnant at a very young age may have a weak protective effect but there are many reasons why delaying pregnancy may be more important.

Risk and health factors that we can change

Life style factors

Life style changes have been shown to reduce the chance of developing heart attacks, strokes and some cancers. Stopping smoking definitely reduces the chance of getting lung cancer but has little to do with breast cancer risk. Some studies indicate that regular exercise (four hours or more per week) during a woman's teens and twenties reduces her chance of getting breast cancer later. It is not known why this happens, whether it is due to changes in hormone levels which occur with vigorous exercise, athletes' eating habits or perhaps the different amounts of body fat carried by active and inactive women. This area requires further study, but several hours per week of regular exercise is to be encouraged.

Stress has many different meanings and personal interpretations but usually involves a sense of loss of control or low self-esteem. Making positive changes to reduce your personal level of stress can have substantial health benefits.

Diet

Diet is clearly an important factor in the development of breast cancer and is something which you can change. However, there is no simple remedy to prevent breast cancer in spite of what one reads on the newsstands. A healthy diet would consist of reducing your total amount of calories eaten and reducing the proportion of calories taken as fat to between 20% and 30% of your total calorie intake. This can be achieved by trimming the visible fat from meat, using leaner cuts, avoiding chocolate, avoiding sauces rich in fat or cream, and substituting low fat milk products (skim or 1%) for the higher fat alternatives. Increasing the amount of green and yellow vegetables, which contain vitamin A, and the fiber content of the diet is to be encouraged (see Chapter 35). It is generally felt that drinking less alcohol may be beneficial, but it is not known how much is safe or is too much. A glass of wine a few times per week is probably still reasonable. Ongoing studies are testing whether dietary restrictions later in life can reduce the chance of developing breast cancer.

No specific dietary therapy can guarantee that breast cancer will not develop. Vegetarians also get breast cancer. However, diet is something over which you do have control: make the most of this power, but don't make yourself miserable! It is important to be prudent, enjoy variety and to maintain balance.

Several recent cookbooks provide tasty, interesting, yet simple menus with attention to a new 'lean' life style (see Additional Reading).

Hormones

Moderate use of oral contraceptives and postmenopausal estrogens (over a period of five to ten years) probably has more advantages with respect to general health than disadvantages in terms of breast cancer risk. It is important to remember that the whole person needs to be considered, not just the risk of breast cancer on its own.

Tamoxifen, an 'anti-estrogen' drug, is used to fight some types of breast cancer (see Chapter 30). Women who take tamoxifen as treatment for breast cancer have a reduced chance of getting a new cancer of the opposite breast. This has led to studies in Europe and North America to test if tamoxifen can safely prevent breast cancer in volunteer women who do not have breast cancer but are at high risk of getting the disease. Until the results of these studies are available, tamoxifen is not recommended as treatment to prevent the development of breast cancer except when participating in a carefully controlled study. What we do recommend is to reduce postmenopausal estrogen and oral contraceptive use to less than 10 years where feasible.

Surgical prevention

Rarely, a family may have breast cancer in three or more generations with several members of each generation affected. These families may benefit from special genetic counselling. Much research is now aimed at identifying specific genes that will indicate which women in these families have an extremely high risk of developing breast cancer. The structure of one such gene, called 'BRCA1' was discovered in 1994. Women who have inherited this gene generally have many cases of breast and ovary cancer in their extended families, and have an 80% chance of developing breast cancer and a 45% chance of developing ovary cancer. Another gene, BRCA2, has also been identified. The presence of this gene indicates a high risk of breast cancer but not ovary cancer. This field of medicine and science is changing rapidly.

Surgical prevention (removal of both breasts) is a drastic measure that should be considered only by women with a very high risk (50% or higher) of getting breast cancer and who have participated in counselling and weighed the alternatives carefully. This procedure is called 'prophylactic mastectomy.'

If both breasts are to be removed as a preventive measure, then the nipples and all the underlying breast tissue should be removed. However, it is not necessary to take out the lymph nodes. Unfortunately, 100% of the breast glands can never be removed so a small risk of developing breast cancer will still remain. 'Subcutaneous mastectomy' is a procedure in which the breast tissue is cut out through a small incision under each breast but the nipple and skin of the breast are not removed. Studies have shown that this procedure actually leaves behind nearly 15% of the breast tissue, so the risk of breast cancer is not eliminated. The cosmetic effect of reconstruction is as good or better after bilateral (both breasts) total mastectomy than after bilateral subcutaneous mastectomy. If the decision is taken to use a surgical approach to breast cancer prevention, eliminating as much of the breast tissue as possible is the goal, so total mastectomy is preferred.

Routine Methods
for Detecting Cancer

CHAPTER SIX

Screening mammography and self-examination can mean early detection

What is screening?

SCREENING IS THE USE OF A TEST or examination in someone who appears well, in other words, with no symptoms, to detect a disease at an early stage. With breast cancer, the goal of screening is to detect a cancer that is so small that it hasn't had a chance to spread yet. Hopefully, treatment will be less radical at this stage and will give a better chance of a cure. For example, if a woman's cancer is found when it is smaller than 1.0 cm in diameter and has not spread to the lymph nodes, it can be treated with a simple operation that leaves the breast intact and she has a better than 95% chance of being cured.

A small cancer means a better chance of cure

A 'small' breast cancer refers to a lump less than 1 to 1.5 cm in diameter (about the width of your little finger) that has not spread to the lymph nodes in the armpit (Figure 7). Cancers of this size are often too small to feel in a normal breast. If not seen on a breast x-ray (mammogram), it may take two to five years to show up as a lump that a woman or her doctor can feel.

Figure 7: A 6 mm invasive cancer was detected on a screening mammogram (arrows). This cancer might have taken another three to five years before it could be felt. This woman was treated by an operation that saved the breast and her chances of being cured are greater than 95%.

Breast cancers detected and treated effectively at this 'small' size have an excellent chance of being completely cured.

Once a cancer is larger than 2.0 cm there is a higher chance that it has already spread to the lymph nodes or elsewhere in the body. A woman with a 3.0 cm tumor, even if it hasn't spread to her lymph nodes, has a 25% chance of developing a recurrence within five years; a woman with a 3.0 cm tumor that has spread to two lymph nodes at the time of diagnosis has a 50% chance of developing more cancer within five years. Therefore, early detection provides a very real hope for increasing the chance of cure and reducing the number of deaths due to breast cancer.

A 3-step plan for early detection

Effective early detection includes a three-pronged approach that requires the woman's participation. She must take responsibility for learning and performing regular breast self-examination, for having an annual physical examination done by a trained health professional, and having mammography done if she is in the appropriate age category. These three parts are all necessary — no single approach can detect all the cancers and each assesses the breast in a different way.

Breast self-examination: any CHANGE is important

Most breast lumps are not cancerous. Many women develop an occasional non-cancerous (benign) lump in the breast that disappears after the next menstrual cycle. Others have a pattern of lumpiness which is normal. What must be detected are CHANGES in the breasts.

The best way to detect changes is for each woman to get to know her own breasts. You learn what is 'normal' by doing a regular breast self-examination every month. For pre-menopausal women this is best done four to six days after the menstrual period ends. For women who are not menstruating, the breast does not change cyclically, so it doesn't matter what day of the month the breasts are checked. The simplest thing to do is to pick a certain day of the month (for example your birthday) and always do the examination on that day each month.

A breast self-examination (Figure 8) should start by simply looking at your breasts in a mirror to see if there are any changes in the skin or the nipple. Good lighting is important. Put your hands on your hips and press your hips to contract the muscles under the breasts and look again for any changes. Pay special attention to the skin surface. Look for unusual swelling, skin puckering, discoloration or nipple changes. Then, still in front of the mirror, swing both arms above the head and watch the breasts to look for changes.

The next part of the examination is to feel your breasts. This is best done when you are relaxed and lying on your back with one hand raised behind your head. A good time would be in bed or in the bathtub. Remember, the breast occupies a large area on the chest: it extends almost up to the collarbone and has a part that reaches into the armpit. When feeling your breasts, use the right hand to feel the left breast and left hand to feel the right breast.

Feel every portion of the breast tissue by holding the fingers together to form a small sensitive area. Do not pinch the breast between your fingers and thumb. A normal breast always feels lumpy if it is pinched. Using the flat part of your fingers, press just firmly enough to feel the ribs but not so hard that it hurts. Use a circular motion. Check for any differences of texture or

Figure 8: Breast self-examination technique.

Standing, arms down, to
check basic appearance

Raising arms to look for changes

Using finger pads in circular motion to feel breast

Lying flat on the back and feeling breast again

Lying slightly to each side to feel breast

lumps that are unusual. Divide the breast into four quarters and examine each quarter one by one to be sure that you examine the whole breast. Squeezing the nipples to look for discharge can be part of the examination but it is not essential. Most discharges are not significant and most women have a little clear or whitish discharge.

Once you have felt each breast, concentrate on carefully feeling the armpits where the lymph nodes are located. A new breast lump or an enlarged lymph node should be checked by your doctor.

Breast self-examination is difficult to learn from a pamphlet or by reading a chapter like this. It is best taught on a 'one-to-one' basis. Your family doctor or surgeon should be able to teach you breast self-examination. The Cancer Society, community health nurses and some breast screening centers conduct teaching sessions. You can call the Cancer Society regional office nearest you for further information.

How good is breast self-examination for detecting cancers?

Despite the fact that many breast cancers are discovered by the woman herself, so far, studies have not shown that breast self-examination prevents cancer deaths. This may be partly because most women do not do breast self-examination regularly and do not know how to do it effectively.

Even so, regular breast self-examination is still recommended because some cancers will be found earlier (Figure 9) and treatment may be more effective. Breast self-examination will also give you knowledge about the normal texture of your breasts. New lumps that don't go away should be brought to the attention of your doctor. If you are familiar with your own body you will be confident that a lump is new and can insist that it be taken seriously.

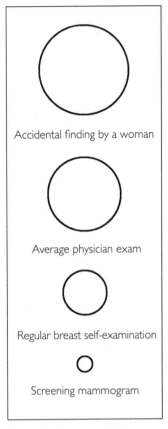

Accidental finding by a woman

Average physician exam

Regular breast self-examination

Screening mammogram

Figure 9: Size at which cancer can be found.

Mammography

What is a mammogram?

A mammogram is a low-dose x-ray of the breast. The dose of radiation is approximately 0.15 centigray (rads) which is about one-fifth the dose of a chest x-ray. It is used very widely for screening large numbers of women who have no symptoms, and it is also used to help diagnose cancer in women who have a suspicious lump (see Chapter 9).

How is a mammogram taken?

The woman stands directly in front of the mammogram machine and the breast is held between two plastic plates

Figure 10: The breast is held between two plates when a mammogram is taken.

(Figure 10). The machine passes x-rays through the breast and onto an x-ray film. Just like the film in a camera, after the picture is taken the mammogram film is then developed. This developed film is 'the mammogram.' The mixed shades of grey, white and black can be interpreted by a radiologist to give information about the inside of the breast (Figure 7).

When the mammogram is taken, the breast is spread out to get a better view of all the tissues in the breast. Unfortunately the pressure on the breast may be uncomfortable but it is brief, about 20 seconds. If this compression causes you severe pain, speak to the technologist taking your mammogram: more gradual compression may help. To reduce the discomfort as much as possible, avoid having the mammogram in the 10 days or week before your period when breast cysts may be more tender.

Does screening with mammography reduce deaths from breast cancer?

Yes for women between 50 and 70 years old

There is strong evidence that mammographic screening for breast cancer can reduce the breast cancer death rate by 25 to 30% for women between 50 and 70 years old. This means that women in this age group are strongly encouraged to have a screening mammogram every year.

No for women younger than 40

Screening healthy women under 40 has not been shown to result in any benefit. One explanation is that the incidence of cancer is low at this age. Another reason may be related to the fact that breast cancers are more difficult to see on an x-ray when they are buried in the type of breast tissue typically found in younger women. As mentioned in Chapter 1, the breast tissue of a 30-year-old woman consists mostly of milk ducts and glands. However, as women age this tissue is replaced by fat, and the breasts of elderly women are made up mostly of fat. Because fat is less dense than ducts and glands, it is easier to identify a tiny developing cancer on the mammogram of an older woman with fatty breasts. Figure 11 compares a typical mammogram of the breast of a 35-year-old woman with that of a 63-year-old woman. Clearly, the tiny new breast cancer (lower) would be more difficult to distinguish from the denser glandular breast tissue of the younger woman (upper).

Yes for healthy women over 70

Although there is not much data regarding the value of screening for women older than 70 years, we recommend its use if a woman has no other serious health problems because breast cancer is quite frequent at this age, and these women may still benefit from the early detection of a breast cancer. Screening mammography may continue to be worthwhile in healthy older women even to the age of 80 years.

'Possibly' for women 40 to 49 years old

We believe that women aged between 40 to 49 years may benefit from screening mammography. Studies have shown a modest decrease in the number of breast cancer deaths in this age group: 13% after 12 years of taking annual mammograms. This difference is small enough that it could have arisen by chance alone. Experts disagree on how to interpret this information and on how strongly to encourage screening mammo-

Figure 11: A comparison of mammograms from a 35-year-old woman (upper) and a 63-year-old woman (lower). The small cancer in the central part of the older woman's breast (arrow) would not have been visible in the younger woman's normal breast.

grams for these women. Because the incidence of cancer is low in this age group it means that many mammograms will need to be done on healthy women before the curable cancers are found. Inclusion of the 40- to 49-year-old group in formal mammography screening programs will increase the 'cost per year of life saved.' However, when making calculations of this nature one must assume that one can place a monetary value on a year of life for women of different ages. If women in this age group are going to seek out mammography, though, they should be allowed to participate in formal screening programs where meticulous attention to quality control of the performance and interpretation of the mammograms can be ensured.

Problems related to screening by mammography

Not all cancers show up on a mammogram

This is a very important point. Up to 10% of breast cancers do not show up on the breast x-ray. There are several reasons for this. Sometimes the breast tissue is so dense that it hides the cancer on the x-ray, other times the cancer may be in such an unusual area of the breast that it is outside of the area that is x-rayed, and sometimes the signs of cancer are so slight that the radiologist misinterprets the film. Of course, the problem with this is that after a 'normal' screening mammogram a woman may be falsely reassured that a lump that she feels is not really a cancer. However, breast lumps should not be ignored just because a mammogram is reported to be 'normal.' It still requires serious investigation.

A 'suspicious' mammogram means fear and worry

Of 1,000 women who have a screening mammogram, about four will be found to have cancer. However, before these four are diagnosed, about 70 will be thought to have an abnormal mammogram. These 70 women will undergo further tests, and perhaps 10 to 15 will have a test called a 'biopsy' where a small piece of the breast is removed and examined under the microscope to determine if it is cancer or not (see Chapter 11). Until the four who actually have cancers are identified, all 70 women will endure a lot of anxiety and fear of having breast cancer.

42

Furthermore, the women whose biopsies are non-cancerous may be thought of as having had surgery 'unnecessarily' during the process of finding the four women who do have cancer.

Does mammography itself cause breast cancer?

Since mammography is a type of x-ray there is a certain amount of exposure to radiation, and the fear of causing cancers by taking mammograms of healthy women needs to be addressed. The amount of radiation used is very small, and the chance of getting cancer from radiation becomes less as we get older. Therefore, the actual risk of getting breast cancer from a mammogram is extremely small, probably lower than one cancer for every one to two million women screened. In contrast, about 4,000 to 8,000 cancers are detected for every one to two million women screened. This means that the benefits of having a mammogram every one to two years, especially for women aged 50 to 70 years, are far greater than any risk from radiation exposure.

Other screening methods that have been considered

Although mammography is not 100% accurate, it is still the best test available for detecting 'small' breast cancers. Other tests that have been considered as screening methods include ultrasound, thermography, transillumination, CAT scan and magnetic resonance imaging. Ultrasound, thermography and transillumination have not proven to be as good as mammography in detecting tiny cancers. CAT scan and magnetic resonance imaging, while as accurate as mammography, are much more expensive and time-consuming.

SECTION FOUR

What Do I Do When I Find A Lump?

CHAPTER SEVEN

A *visit to the doctor*

Finding a lump

THE DISCOVERY OF A NEW BREAST LUMP understandably causes tremendous anxiety, but it may help to know that most lumps, nearly 80%, are benign (not cancerous). However, noticing a lump is often the first sign that may lead to a diagnosis of breast cancer. It is important to show any new lump or other breast abnormality to your doctor — and you should expect that it will be looked at in some detail.

What happens when I show the lump to a doctor?

The doctor will ask when you first noticed the lump and whether it has changed, especially in relation to your menstrual cycle. Any previous breast problems and risk factors will be discussed, including biopsies, infections or injuries, and facts regarding your menstrual cycle, use of medications or hormones, and your family history (health of family members).

It is best to examine the breasts of a premenopausal woman a week or two after the menstrual period, but if there is a worrisome lump you should not delay that first visit. During the breast examination you and the doctor are usually alone in the examining room, but you can certainly request the presence of

47

a nurse or bring a family member or friend along for moral support and as a 'second set of ears' to help remember what has been said.

You will be asked to disrobe at least the upper half of your body. Depending on your physician's judgement, you may have a partial or complete physical examination. This may include listening to your chest and examining the lymph node areas in your neck and armpits, both breasts and the abdomen. A pelvic examination is part of a yearly health exam and may be done but it is not essential to the diagnosis of breast cancer.

What happens next?

Depending on what the doctor thinks about the abnormality you may need no further tests. The doctor's recommendation will depend partly on your age. This is a factor that greatly affects the risk of getting breast cancer (Chapter 4). If you are in your teens, the breast lump is almost certainly benign: breast cancer is very rare in this age group. If you are in your twenties, the vast majority of lumps are benign, but an occasional case of breast cancer is seen every year. In the thirties and forties, breast cancer becomes more frequent, and among postmenopausal women there is a substantial possibility that a new breast lump is cancerous.

If some tests are needed, they may be done in the office or you may be sent for a mammogram, ultrasound or other tests. Assessment of your particular breast problem may require consultation with a surgeon, or you may need a biopsy, which involves surgical removal of a small piece of breast tissue for further examination (see Chapter 11).

CHAPTER EIGHT

Breast lumps and other signs of trouble

Breast cysts

MANY WOMEN HAVE PAIN, lumpiness and swelling of the breasts one to two weeks before their menstrual period begins. This is due to hormones in the breast glands that cause fluid-filled lumps called 'cysts' to become swollen and tight. Such cysts are rarely associated with cancer, in other words, they are benign.

Fibrocystic disease

This condition is so common that many doctors feel it should not be called a 'disease' at all, just a 'variation of normal.' Fibrocystic breasts have areas of fibrosis (scarring) and cysts (enlarged milk glands) which cause lumpiness of the breasts that may come and go with the body's normal hormone changes.

As a rule, fibrocystic disease is only associated with a higher chance of developing breast cancer if the cells lining the cysts or ducts show excessive cell growth (hyperplasia) and an abnormal appearance under the microscope (atypia). Chapter 2 gives a more detailed description of atypia and hyperplasia.

Other breast changes not related to cancer

Sclerosing adenosis

Sclerosing adenosis means that there is a lot of scarring and inflammation around the breast glands. This condition may show up as fine calcifications on a mammogram.

Duct ectasia

Duct ectasia refers to widened (or dilated) milk ducts. This is often seen in women who have had surgery for nipple discharge. The dilated ducts can become filled with dead cells and fluids, and may bleed or become infected.

Papillomas

Papillomas are small growths inside the milk ducts. They are benign, but may cause bleeding from the nipple.

Apocrine metaplasia

Apocrine metaplasia means that the milk duct cells have a different appearance when looked at under a microscope. It is not related to cancer in any way, nor is it a reason for concern, but it may be mentioned in a 'pathology report' of a breast biopsy (see Chapter 13).

Fibroadenomas

Fibroadenomas are firm, round, fibrous lumps that are most often found in young women.

Fat necrosis

Fat necrosis refers to a lump of dead fat cells in the breast. This condition may occur after an injury severe enough to cause bruising: after a car accident, physical abuse or sometimes after surgery. A minor bump or a bra that rubs does not cause fat necrosis, so if a tender lump is noticed after a minor injury it needs to be fully checked to be sure that it is not caused by cancer.

Breast infections

Breast infections are unusual except in women who are breastfeeding. In general, infections are treated easily with antibiotics. However, it is important to realize that a woman who is NOT breastfeeding and notices a red, swollen or tender breast may be showing signs of cancer, and a biopsy should be considered.

Signs that may indicate cancer

Breast lumps

Today, with increasing use of screening mammography, many cancers are found before they can be felt. However, women still often find the lump themselves. Sometimes it happens during the regular breast self-examination, but more often it occurs just by accident. There is no particular 'feel' to a cancerous lump but some women say that they 'knew' it was 'different' from other lumps they had felt in the past. Cancer lumps are usually firm or hard and, although they are usually painless, they may be tender. Sometimes women first notice a lump in the armpit — an enlarged lymph node. Lumps that feel as though they are attached to the skin or also have skin redness are especially likely to be cancerous.

Nipple changes

Crusting, ulceration or eczema (weeping) of the nipple that does not go away in a few days may be the result of breast cancer cells growing into the nipple. This can be due to cancer or to another condition called Paget's disease in which cancer cells grow between the skin cells of the nipple (see Chapter 14). If the nipple becomes inverted (turns inward) it may be a sign of a growing cancer pulling on the ligaments of the breast as it enlarges.

Discharge from the nipple

A small amount of clear or whitish discharge can be squeezed from the nipple of most women and is NOT a cause for concern. Nipple discharge may occur on its own and may be white, yellow or even green. Although this is unusual it is almost always due to a benign condition.

Sometimes the discharge may be bloody. Although this is usually due to a small, benign papilloma in one of the milk ducts, sometimes an early cancer may show up this way.

Nipple discharge, especially with bleeding, should be investigated by your doctor and may require surgical removal of the bleeding milk duct.

Changing breast size and skin changes

Any new change of the breast should be evaluated, especially if it happens only on one side. This may be as simple a change as one breast becoming larger, or dimpling, redness or thickening of the skin or the nipple. These changes are particularly worrisome because they may indicate that cancer has already spread and is blocking the drainage of the breast tissues to the lymph nodes.

CHAPTER NINE

Diagnostic mammography

What is a mammogram and how is it taken?

THESE ASPECTS ARE EXPLAINED in detail in Chapter 6 and illustrated in Figures 10 (p. 39) and 12 (p. 54).

Several images are often taken

When a new lump is found, a mammogram should be taken of BOTH breasts to get information about the extent and type of the abnormality. By 'flattening' each breast first horizontally and then vertically within the plastic plates of the mammogram machine, the mammograms will show the breast from different angles and provide more information. Figure 12 shows two views of the same breast. Additional views may be taken to highlight parts of the breast that look suspicious or are not seen completely in the standard views. For example, an image may be taken to focus on the extreme outside part of the breast.

In addition, a 'magnification view' can be used to get a close-up image of an area of concern (Figure 13). These magnification views are taken with special compression plates. Many apparent masses are due to breast glands lying on top of each other — such overlapping glands are pressed apart during compression. If a mass disappears when it is compressed, it is not a cancer.

Figure 12: Localizing a breast abnormality requires two views. The first image (B) was made by passing x-rays from top to bottom through the breast (A). The second image (D) was made by passing the x-rays from side to side through the breast (C). The arrow identifies the cancer on the mammograms B and D.

A mass that keeps its shape is probably real and the possibility that it contains a cancer needs to be assessed further.

Signs of cancer on a mammogram

As mentioned in Chapter 6 on screening mammography, it is important to emphasize that approximately 10% of cancers do not show up on a mammogram, even when a lump can be felt. There is no single feature on a mammogram that always indicates cancer. However, three features commonly indicate its presence: an irregular dense area not seen in the opposite breast (Figure 13), clusters of irregular, tiny, white areas that indicate calcium deposits, and thickening of the overlying skin, possibly due to cancerous invasion.

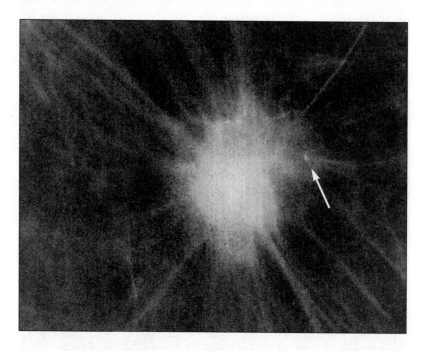

Figure 13: A close-up view shows more detail. The cancer identified in Figure 12 is shown in a 'magnification' view which gives a more detailed 'close-up' view of the abnormality. The thin white streaks extending from the main body of the cancer are 'arms' or tentacles of cancer growing out into the tissues. The small, irregular, very dense white spot (arrow) is a calcium deposit inside a milk duct that is cancerous.

There are many possible reasons, other than cancer, for lumps or calcium deposits on a mammogram. If a lump or calcium deposit is very smooth and round or unchanged for several years, it is not likely to be due to cancer and doesn't need to be removed (Figure 14). However, if an abnormality is new or irregular it should be removed to check if a cancer is present. Therefore, careful interpretation is necessary, and radiologists may seek second opinions from a colleague before recommending a biopsy.

Other information from the mammogram

How big is the lump or cancer?

The mammogram can give information about the size of the lump or cancer. Calcifications, for instance, can sometimes be seen to extend many centimeters from the lump that you actually feel. If the lump turns out to be cancer, this information will be very important in making the decision whether it is feasible

Figure 14: The calcifications (arrow) seen in this mammogram are round and smooth and have been present and unchanged for several years. They are benign and do not need to be removed.

Figure 15: Mammograms of both breasts were used to evaluate the lump felt by a 68-year-old woman in the upper part of her left breast (left). The dense area in the right breast (right; arrow) could not be felt but was also removed and found to be a 1.2 cm diameter invasive cancer.

to save the breast. It is important, therefore, to have a mammogram to obtain this information before a biopsy is done because the breast may feel too bruised or sore to obtain a mammogram after the biopsy.

Is there another 'hidden' cancer?

If one cancer is found it is also important to check the rest of the breast and the breast on the opposite side to make sure that an additional hidden (occult) cancer is not missed. Figure 15 shows the mammograms of a woman who found a single lump in the left breast. A cancer too small to be felt was found on the mammogram of the opposite breast. One or two women in 100 who are diagnosed with cancer will be found to have a cancer in the other breast at the same time.

What are the limitations of mammograms?

As explained above, the main problem with mammograms is that about one out of every 10 cancers does not show up. What this means is that if a new lump can be felt but a mammogram is read as 'normal,' unfortunately there is no cause for reassurance. The lump may have been too far to one side to show up on the film, the cancer may have been missed because it looked too similar to the rest of the breast, or the films, although abnormal, may have been misinterpreted.

Another limitation is that although an abnormality may look very much like a cancer or, alternatively, very much like a benign condition, the mammogram alone does not provide enough information to make the diagnosis. The diagnosis must be finalized with a biopsy (an examination of cells from the lump or the abnormal area).

CHAPTER TEN

Diagnostic ultrasound

What is an ultrasound?

AN ULTRASOUND USES SOUND WAVES to assess the breast. This method does not use x-rays. In other words, no radiation is involved.

The ultrasound machine includes a small hand-held device that is held directly against the skin while the sound waves are transmitted painlessly through the breast. You will feel a small vibration. Lubricating jelly is put on the skin to transmit the sound waves better to the skin surface. This jelly is a bit messy but washes off easily.

The sound waves are transmitted through the breast tissue and bounce back to the ultrasound machine. The machine then converts the pattern of rebounding sound waves into images which show up on a television monitor as images of the different tissues of the breast.

What does ultrasound show?

The main use of ultrasound is to find out if a lump in the breast is either solid (more likely to be cancerous), or a cyst (filled with fluid and very unlikely to be cancerous).

Ultrasound may be used to provide additional information to that on the mammogram. If a mass on the mammogram is suspicious but unclear, the ultrasound may be able to show if the mass is a cyst or solid, and this will help to decide whether the area should be removed.

Ultrasound can also be used to direct a needle into a suspicious breast lump so that cells can be removed to be examined under the microscope. This is called an ultrasound-guided needle biopsy.

Ultrasound is not useful for screening healthy women in the hope of detecting early cancers: mammography is better at distinguishing the small cancers. Also, the small calcifications which are often the earliest sign of cancer on a mammogram are not visible on an ultrasound.

CHAPTER ELEVEN

Fine needle aspirations and biopsies

What is a biopsy and when is it needed?

IN MANY CASES THE MAMMOGRAMS and ultrasound (see Chapters 9 and 10) give enough information to diagnose a benign condition in the breast and no further tests are necessary. However, if the diagnosis is still uncertain, then the next step is to take some breast tissue from the suspicious area and look at it under a microscope. The process of removing the cells or tissue is called 'taking a biopsy.' There are several ways to do this, some of which are quick and relatively painless, and others which are more complicated and require surgery.

A needle biopsy

A needle biopsy (or fine-needle aspiration biopsy) can be done in the doctor's office. It takes only a few seconds and usually causes no more pain than having a blood test. The skin may or may not be 'frozen' with a local anesthetic. Then, while holding the lump between two fingers, the surgeon or pathologist uses a syringe with a very thin needle to suck some material from the lump (Figure 16).

Figure 16: A needle biopsy involves the use of a needle to remove some material from the lump.

If the lump is a cyst

If the lump is a cyst, the fluid in the cyst will be drawn into the syringe and the lump will disappear. No further action may be necessary!

The vast majority of cysts are benign. The cyst fluid may be a wide range of colors: clear, green, white, yellow, etc. Since little information can be obtained from this fluid it is usually thrown away. If the cyst fluid is bloody or if the lump remains even after all the fluid has been drained, there is cause for concern. In these cases, surgery is needed because there may be a cancer that is producing the cyst fluid or the lump. Also, if a cyst appears benign but keeps coming back after several aspirations (removal of fluid by needle), a surgical biopsy may be wise.

If the lump is solid

If the lump is solid, small clumps of cells (invisible to the naked eye) will be sucked into the needle. These cells are smeared onto slides and then prepared for the microscope. The preparation and interpretation of the slides may take from one to seven days.

Based on this microscopic examination of the cells the diagnosis of cancer is quite accurate: if the report comes back as 'positive for cancer' the diagnosis is correct 95% to 97% of the time. However, if the report is 'negative for cancer' or 'non-diagnostic,' it could just mean that the cancer was missed by the needle or that cancer cells, although present, were not sucked out during the aspiration. At least 15% of breast cancers can be missed by the needle biopsy. Therefore, if the lump is solid or looks suspicious, a 'negative' or 'non-diagnostic' report should be ignored and a surgical biopsy should be done.

A core biopsy

For a core biopsy, a needle is used to obtain a small core of tissue about 2 mm in diameter and 1 to 3 cm in length. This is also called a 'Tru-cut biopsy.' After a local anesthetic is injected, a small 'nick' is made in the skin and a large needle is pushed into the breast while the surgeon holds the lump. This method may be uncomfortable or painful for the patient and requires the use of a special cutting-needle apparatus but provides much more tissue for examination than a needle aspiration biopsy. A core biopsy is usually obtained from a palpable mass. Some centers have a special apparatus attached to a mammogram machine that enables core biopsies of non-palpable lumps to be obtained. The core biopsy needle is advanced to the correct depth under computer-directed control. This technique is called 'stereotactic core needle biopsy' (see Chapter 12).

A surgical (open) biopsy

A surgical biopsy or open biopsy involves making a small cut or incision in the skin of the breast and cutting out a piece of breast tissue (Figure 17). This may take place at the doctor's office or in a hospital, and can be done under a local or a general anesthetic.

Excisional biopsy: the whole lump is taken out

In addition to removing the entire lump, a small rim of the surrounding normal breast tissue is also removed. This leaves a small scar, but unless the lump was huge it should not form a defect in the shape of the breast. Although such a biopsy can be a frightening experience, it is actually quite a simple surgical procedure.

Incisional biopsy: only a part of the lump is removed

Using anesthetic, the surgeon makes an incision through the skin and removes only a small part of the lump rather than the whole thing. This is done only when a lump is very large and when an excisional biopsy would cause a severe breast deformity or would not remove all of the cancer anyway. For example, when a cancer has invaded the skin or the chest wall, the doctor may do an incisional biopsy to confirm the diagnosis of cancer before discussing treatment options.

Other considerations

Although the biopsy may remove the whole mass, this is just the first step in the treatment plan. The surgeon who will be

Figure 17: An open biopsy involves making a small cut in the skin and cutting out a piece of breast tissue.

responsible for the final, curative operation on the breast, if needed, should be the one to do the biopsy. The advantage is that the surgeon can assess the breast carefully and plan the position of the biopsy scar in such a way that it will fit with any additional surgery. The incision should always be placed to give the best cosmetic result and to make as little change in the shape of the breast as possible. The length of the biopsy scar will depend on the size of the lump, but it should not be more than a few centimeters long.

Whichever type of surgical biopsy is done, the specimen is sent directly to the pathologist for a number of studies. If the lump is obviously cancerous, a piece is processed immediately for testing the hormone receptor content (this is related to treatment; see Chapter 30). However, the main part of the biopsy tissue is processed for a detailed examination under the microscope (see Chapter 13).

A *frozen section biopsy*

In some situations a quick decision must be made about treatment while in the operating room, and a 'frozen section' or 'rush section' is done. This means that a piece of breast tissue is frozen while the patient is still on the operating table and ultrathin slices of the tissue are examined under the microscope. This takes about 10 to 20 minutes. The problem with this method is that it is neither as good nor as complete as the diagnosis made when the pathologist has more time to examine the entire tissue sample and look at sections from several different areas of the tissue. The diagnosis of cancer inside the milk ducts can be especially difficult to make on a frozen section.

One situation where the frozen section is often done is to confirm a needle biopsy report that is 'positive for cancer' before the surgeon proceeds with the actual operation to remove the cancer (mastectomy or lumpectomy and axillary dissection). As mentioned earlier, the positive needle biopsy is correct 95% to 97% of the time, but this means that in 3% to 5% of cases it is wrong, in other words, the lump is actually benign, and no surgery is needed.

In cases where a diagnosis of cancer has not been made before the operation it is usually best to perform the surgical biopsy and then wait for the pathologist to give a definite diagnosis, even if this takes a few days. Then, decisions about further tests and treatment can be made when the patient is awake and fully able to participate.

Biopsy and curative surgery
Which is best: a 'one step' or 'two step' procedure?

The 'one step procedure' means that the cancer is diagnosed and the curative surgery is done at the same time, usually under one general anesthetic. The surgeon does an excisional biopsy of the tumor and the pathologist does a rush or frozen section to make the diagnosis while the patient is still under anesthetic. If it is cancer, the surgeon continues and does a partial mastectomy and axillary dissection or a modified radical mastectomy, whichever is appropriate (see Chapter 19).

There is no real advantage to having everything done quickly in one procedure, except maybe from a financial standpoint, or for the convenience of the surgeon. There may be disadvantages, as the woman has neither the opportunity to adjust to the diagnosis of cancer, nor does she have any input into the type of surgical procedure that will be used.

The 'two step procedure' is usually preferable. In this case the diagnosis is made first, either from fine-needle aspiration or a surgical (open) biopsy where either the whole lump or part of the lump is removed and a careful diagnosis is made by a pathologist (see Chapter 11). The curative surgery is done as a second step on another day after the pathologist has had time to interpret the specimen. This gives the surgeon and the patient time to discuss treatment options. Since there is no scientific evidence that a short time between diagnosis and surgery is harmful, it gives the patient time to prepare herself physically and emotionally for the next step.

CHAPTER TWELVE

If the screening mammogram is abnormal

What happens if my screening mammogram is abnormal?

IF YOU ARE TOLD THAT your screening mammogram is abnormal do NOT assume that you have cancer! An abnormal result simply means that you need further evaluation to find out if the abnormality is really a cancer or only scarring, cysts or some other problem.

The first step is to go see your doctor and to repeat the physical examination. Sometimes the abnormality can also be felt. Your doctor should compare the new mammogram to other mammograms you may have had previously. A mass that has been present and UNCHANGED for many years does not need to be removed. Often, more mammograms will be taken to provide greater detail of the abnormality (see Chapter 9).

If your doctor cannot feel the lump that is seen on the mammogram, an ultrasound may be used to distinguish between a cyst or a solid mass. Also, a fine-needle aspiration done under ultrasound guidance may provide more information (see Chapter 10).

If, after the physical examination, the mammograms and the ultrasound, the mass in your breast is still 'questionable' it will have to be removed by surgical (open) biopsy so that it can be examined in more detail. However, if the surgeon cannot feel the abnormal area, it becomes difficult to judge how much of the breast to remove. Instead of going in 'blind,' a technique called 'fine-wire localization directed biopsy' can be used to help the surgeon find the exact location of the lump in the breast.

Fine-wire localization biopsy

Before the surgery another mammogram is taken. With the breast still held between the mammographic plates the radiologist locates the abnormality on the mammogram, local anesthetic is applied to the skin, and a hollow needle is inserted into the breast down to the abnormal area. More mammograms are taken to check the position of the needle.

A very fine wire with a tiny hook on the end is threaded down through the hollow needle and the needle is withdrawn, leaving the tiny hook at the end of the wire snagged in the suspicious area. The other end of the fine wire is sticking out of the skin.

The patient is then taken to surgery for the open biopsy and the surgeon can follow the wire to find the area that needs to be removed.

A new biopsy technique

Recently, a new device has become available that in future may avoid many of the surgical biopsies that are now done to check abnormalities found by screening mammography. While the breast is held in place between the plates of a mammogram machine, two x-rays are taken at different angles that allows the precise position of the abnormal area to be located. Then a computerized biopsy 'gun' places a core-biopsy needle exactly into the abnormal area. This technique is called 'stereotactic core-needle biopsy.' However, it remains to be seen whether it will be accurate enough to replace the use of surgical biopsies.

What Type of Cancer Is It?

CHAPTER THIRTEEN

The pathology report: reading the cancer's telltale signs

WHEN A SURGEON REMOVES a suspicious or cancerous lump from the breast, a lot of important information can be gained by looking at the lump itself and examining small bits of it under the microscope (Figures 18 and 19).

In cases where the diagnosis is uncertain, this detailed examination of the breast lump or tissue establishes whether cancer is present or not. In situations where the diagnosis of cancer has already been made, it provides information that helps predict how the cancer will behave in the future. Is it likely to grow back? Where? When? Armed with this information, a treatment strategy can be planned with the goal of blocking the cancer's attempts to grow back and increasing your chance of being cured. The physician who specializes in the study of tissues is referred to as a pathologist, and the pathologist's written summary is called the pathology report.

The three sections of the pathology report

The pathology report contains three main sections: the gross (as seen with the naked eye) description of the tissues, the microscopic description, and the summary (final diagnosis).

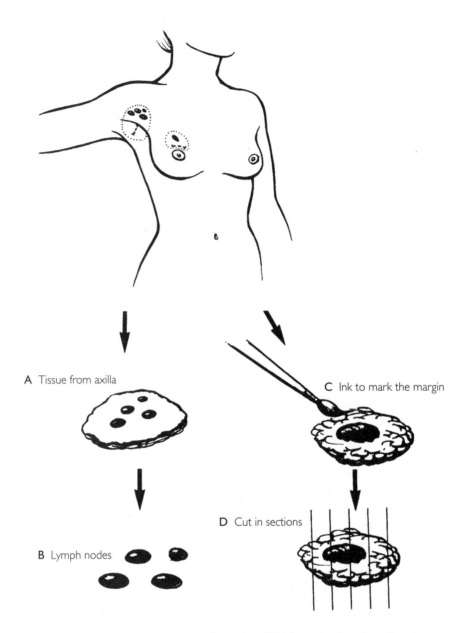

Figure 18: Tissue from the axillary dissection (A) is examined and any lymph nodes are removed and counted (B). The external surface of the breast tissue containing the cancer is painted with ink (C) and then the specimen is cut into sections (D).

Figure 19: Preparation of a small piece of the breast lump for viewing on a microscope slide.

The gross (as seen with the naked eye) description of the tissues

The pathologist reports on what he or she can see with the naked eye: the size of the lump, and the number and size of any lymph nodes. It is then noted how close the cancer is to the edge of the specimen. This is important: if the cancer is right against the edge rather than being centered within a block of normal-looking tissue, the surgeon has cut too closely to the cancer and there is a high likelihood that some of the cancer was left behind in the breast. If the cancer is large enough, a piece is immediately frozen and saved for later testing for estrogen and/or progesterone receptor levels (Chapter 30). Once samples are cut for microscopic examination, the remaining tissue is immersed in a container of formaldehyde and labelled with your name. Specimens are stored like this for years in case further examination is required.

The microscopic description

Under the microscope, breast cancer cells look different from normal cells. The pathologist will write details of the type of cancer, the grade (an assessment of how aggressive the cancer looks), and whether the cancer has invaded the tissues surrounding the main cancer, especially whether cancer cells are seen within the lymph or blood vessels within the breast. Other important features include the presence of dead and dying cells (necrosis), which is a feature of rapidly growing cancers, and the number of mitoses — cells that have been 'caught in the act' of multiplying, which is an indicator of the cancer's growth rate.

If any lymph nodes have been removed from under the arm the pathologist will report on whether the cancer has spread into the lymph nodes. In fact, the report should document how many nodes were found, and how many, if any, were affected by cancer ('involved' or 'positive nodes'). It should also mention whether the cancer has grown through the lymph node and out into the surrounding fat (called an 'extranodal extension').

Final diagnosis

This is a summary of the results of the gross and microscopic examinations. The process of tissue inspection and preparation of this report usually takes anywhere from two to seven days.

The report then becomes a permanent part of the patient's record. The important features which usually influence your doctor's decision about treatment strategy are listed in Table 4.

**Table 4 Features of the pathology report
that affect treatment strategy**

The Tumor

    Size: measured in centimeters

    Type: in situ, invasive, or mixed (see Chapters 14 and 15); ductal, lobular, or other

    Invasion: of the lymphatic, vascular or perineural spaces

    Grade: the degree of aggressiveness

    Number of mitoses: the cancer's growth rate

    Necrosis: in the invasive component of the cancer (a feature of rapidly growing cancers)

    Receptors for estrogen and/or progesterone: see Chapter 30

    Extension of tumor: to skin, to muscle, to excision margins

    Other prognostic markers: p53, oncogenes, c-erb-B2, growth factors, ploidy

The Lymph Nodes

    Total number of lymph nodes recovered

    Number of involved nodes

    Maximum size of involved nodes

    Extranodal extension (growth beyond the lymph nodes): presence or absence

---

CHAPTER FOURTEEN

In situ cancer: Cancer that hasn't invaded or spread

'IN SITU' CANCER IN THE BREAST refers to a cancer that is still within the milk ducts and/or lobules (the milk glands) of the breast. In other words, the cancer cells have not invaded through the walls of the milk ducts; they are in the same place (or *situ*ation) where they first formed.

Ductal carcinoma in situ (DCIS)

The milk ducts become blocked and enlarged as cancer cells accumulate inside them (Figure 20). Calcium tends to collect in the blocked ducts (Figure 21) and is visible on mammograms as tiny white lines and dots (Figure 22). These clusters of fine, irregular calcifications often indicate in situ cancer. If they are present on a mammogram, a biopsy should be done. In situ cancer of the ducts accounts for 10% to 20% of the cancers found by screening mammography. This type of cancer is also referred to as 'intraductal cancer.' Ductal carcinoma in situ, if left untreated, may progress to form an invasive cancer with the potential for spreading throughout the body (Figure 20). In some cases progression can take just a few months, but it usually takes as long as 5 to 10 years.

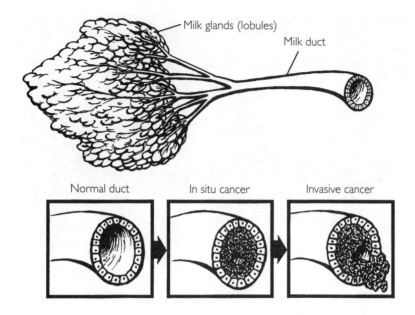

Figure 20: Cross-sectional view of milk duct. The duct may become filled with in situ cancer cells and eventually form an invasive cancer.

Figure 21: Ductal carcinoma in situ cells (large arrow) seen under the microscope. The dark material (small arrow) is a calcium deposit inside the milk duct.

77

Figure 22: Calcium deposits typical of ductal carcinoma in situ as seen on a mammogram.

Ductal carcinoma in situ occurs as two different cell types, with one tending to progress to invasion more quickly than the other. The first type, which progresses more slowly, consists of smaller, more normal-looking cells. These may be called 'solid,' 'papillary' or 'cribiform.' The second type, called 'comedo-carcinoma,' often progresses to invasion early in its growth and consists of large, irregular-shaped cells. It is especially important that comedocarcinomas are treated effectively. Chapter 20 describes the treatment of in situ cancers.

Lobular carcinoma in situ (LCIS)

Lobular carcinoma in situ refers to cancer cells that have formed in the milk glands (as opposed to the milk ducts) and are still confined there. This type of in situ cancer is often found in women around the age of menopause. Lobular carcinoma in situ is different from ductal carcinoma in situ in that there is a high risk that the entire tissue of both breasts may develop cancer. Therefore, treatment of lobular carcinoma in situ

(Chapter 20) must be aimed at both breasts rather than just the affected one, as is the case with ductal carcinoma in situ.

Paget's disease

Paget's disease is a rare form of in situ cancer that can occur in a 'pure' form but it is often accompanied by an invasive cancer. Paget's disease appears as a reddish, itching, scaling or 'eczema' of the nipple caused by cancer cells in the skin of the nipple and areola. Although the traditional treatment is mastectomy, it may be possible to save the breast if there is no underlying invasive cancer. However, the breast must be large enough to tolerate the removal of skin, and the woman needs to accept that there will be a change in sensation and appearance due to the removal of the nipple and areola.

As well as removing the nipple and some surrounding skin, a sample of the breast tissue beneath should also be taken to make sure there is no accompanying invasive cancer. It is not yet clear whether radiation therapy should always follow surgical excision, but in most reports radiation treatment has been added when using a breast-conserving approach for Paget's disease.

The different types
of invasive breast cancer

What is an invasive breast cancer?

CANCER BECOMES 'INVASIVE' when the cancer cells grow through the walls of the milk ducts and glands into the normal fatty tissue of the breast (Figure 20, p. 77). These cells can also be carried elsewhere in the body through the blood stream or lymph system. It is this ability to invade and spread through the body that makes us fear cancer.

Invasive cancers do not grow like an expanding balloon. Rather, finger-like projections of cells grow out into the normal breast tissue from the main cancer. The body often recognizes these cells as foreign and attempts to mount a defense, which causes inflammation and scar tissue to form around the growing cancer. This is what forms the hard lump which is often the first thing a woman notices.

The finger-like projections and scarring can be seen under the microscope and sometimes even on a mammogram. Figure 13 (p. 55) is a picture of a mammogram showing the typical appearance of an invasive cancer.

Microscopic evaluation of the cancer provides information about its likely future behavior (see Box, p. 82) and makes it possible to counsel a woman about her risks, and about the type of treatment that would best improve her chances of cure.

Table 5 **Classification and occurrence of invasive breast cancer***

From ducts and glands	From other parts of the breast
Adenocarcinomas	Cystosarcoma phyllodes (1%)
Ductal carcinoma	Sarcomas (various types)
not otherwise specified (75%)	(less than 1%)
tubular (1%)	Lymphomas (various types)
mucinous (1%)	(less than 1%)
colloid (1%)	
medullary (1%)	
inflammatory (3% to 5%)	
Lobular carcinoma (15%)	
Squamous carcinomas (less than 1%)	
Mixed carcinomas (adenosquamous	
and metaplastic) (less than 1%)	

* Percentages refer to the proportion of women with breast cancer who have the specific subtype.

Common types of invasive breast cancer

Ductal carcinoma

By far the most common type of invasive breast cancer arises from the cells lining the milk ducts. It is called 'ductal carcinoma' or 'ductal adenocarcinoma.' When doctors talk about 'breast cancer' they usually mean ductal carcinoma (see Table 5).

In some women the cell type of ductal carcinoma may vary slightly. These subtypes are referred to as tubular, colloid, mucinous, scirrhous and medullary carcinomas. However, their treatment is usually no different than that of other ductal carcinomas.

Inflammatory carcinomas

Inflammatory carcinoma, which also usually begins in the milk ducts, is a particularly aggressive and rapidly spreading type of breast cancer. Fortunately it does not occur often. The cancer spreads in the lymph channels of the breast and skin, causing the breast to become swollen, enlarged and tender. The skin becomes red and warm so that it may look infected. By the time of diagnosis, inflammatory cancer has almost always spread to the lymph nodes.

Trying to predict the future:
How to predict the behavior of an invasive breast cancer

The chance of a breast cancer spreading and forming cancers in other parts of the body (metastases) can be estimated based on certain features of the cancer: its size, lymph node involvement, lymphatic or blood vessel invasion, cancer grade and other factors (see also Chapter 17).

Tumor Size

The larger the cancer, the more likely it has (or will) spread. Breast cancers are classified as 'small' if they are less than two cm in diameter, 'medium' if two to five cm in diameter, and 'large' if bigger than five cm. No matter what size the cancer, if it is invading the skin or growing into the chest wall, muscles or bones it is said to be 'locally advanced' and has a fairly high risk of recurrence and spread.

Number of Cancerous Lymph Nodes

The risk of cancer spreading increases according to the number of axillary (armpit) lymph nodes found to have cancer. If the patient is treated by surgery alone, the chance of the cancer spreading and reappearing within five to ten years is: 30% to 50% if one to three lymph nodes are cancerous; 50% to 75% if four to nine lymph nodes are cancerous; and 75% or higher if ten or more lymph nodes have cancer.

Lymphatic or Blood Vessel Invasion

If cancer cells are found in the lymph channels or blood vessels in the breast the prognosis is similar to the situation of having one to three cancerous lymph nodes.

Grade

Depending on the microscopic appearance of the cells, the cancer is classified as grade 1, 2, or 3. A higher grade cancer (grade 3) tends to grow faster and spread earlier than a lower grade one.

Other Features

Other features are less reliable than the above features, but may be used to provide additional information. These include measuring the number of cells 'caught in the act' of dividing, referred to as the 'mitotic index' or the 'percent S-phase' (synthesis phase). Features such as ploidy, p53, c-erb-B2, growth factors, oncogenes and other new tests may be used in some centers as additional predictors of prognosis.

Any woman who appears to have a breast infection (other than mastitis while breastfeeding) should have the condition checked promptly to exclude the possibility of an inflammatory cancer.

Lobular carcinomas

Lobular carcinomas account for approximately 15% of invasive breast cancers. These cancers are virtually always estrogen receptor-positive (Chapter 30) so are quite likely to respond to treatments that involve altering the hormonal balance of the body.

Rare types of invasive breast cancer

Squamous and metaplastic cancers, which also begin in the milk ducts, have a worse prognosis than the usual ductal carcinomas.

Cancers that begin in areas of the breast other than the ducts and glands are very rare and include three main groups: sarcomas, lymphomas and cystosarcoma phyllodes. Sarcomas are tumors of the 'connective tissue' such as the nerves, fat, fibrous tissue or blood vessels in the breast. Lymphomas are tumors of white blood cells and may rarely start in the breast. A detailed discussion of sarcomas and lymphomas is beyond the scope of this book because they are so rare and their behavior and treatment is entirely different from the other breast cancers.

It is often difficult to tell if a cystosarcoma phyllodes is malignant or benign (they are usually benign). The pathologist estimates the possibility of malignancy based on the proportion of cells that are actively dividing (the number of mitoses). Cystosarcoma phyllodes is usually cured by surgical removal of the tumor, either a wide local excision or a mastectomy, depending on the tumor's size and location. Phyllodes tumors may cause problems by regrowing at the original site or regrowing on the chest wall after mastectomy.

PART TWO | What are my options now that I have a diagnosis of breast cancer?

SECTION SIX

An Overview of Treatment

CHAPTER SIXTEEN

An overview of
breast cancer treatment

Is there more than one way to treat breast cancer?

YOU MAY FIND IT CONFUSING to learn that the treatment you've been recommended for breast cancer is quite different from what others have received. An aunt may have had a mastectomy, while a friend was treated with chemotherapy and radiation first followed by mastectomy. Another friend might have had a partial mastectomy and radiation, whereas you may have been advised to have a 'lumpectomy,' radiation and tamoxifen.

Why all these different approaches? What do these different treatments mean? What is the best treatment for you? Part 2 of this book describes the different treatment options and explains why each has certain advantages for different types of breast cancer or for different women.

Figure 23 outlines the usual steps that are followed from the moment cancer is first suspected until arriving at a final treatment plan. This process allows for an individualized approach that will provide the best combination of treatment strategies for your particular situation.

The suspicion of cancer may have arisen from a lump discovered by you or your doctor (Chapter 7), an abnormal screening mammogram (Chapter 12) or some other breast problem.

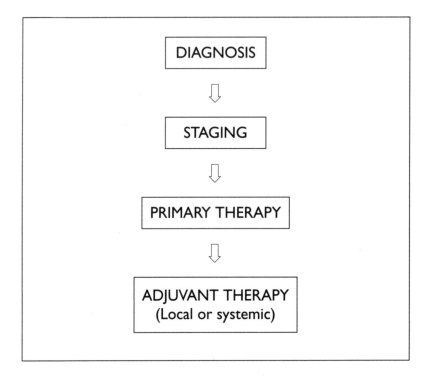

Figure 23: Steps leading to a diagnosis and treatment plan for a woman with breast cancer.

The diagnosis of cancer requires that a piece of breast tissue or a sample of cells be removed and examined by a pathologist (Chapter 13). If a diagnosis of breast cancer is made, tests and examinations will be done to assess the extent (or stage) of disease (Chapter 17).

If the cancer is confined to the breast and lymph nodes in the armpit, as it is in over 90% of cases, then the 'primary therapy,' usually surgery (Chapter 19), is aimed at removing the cancerous tissues. However, new treatments such as 'preoperative chemotherapy' are now being explored (Chapter 27), especially in cases where the tumor is bulky. The important decision about the type of surgery to be used, either mastectomy or an approach that saves the breast, requires your input (Chapter 21).

Once the cancer has been removed, the prognosis of the cancer can be further evaluated by the pathologist's examination of the cancerous tissue (Chapters 13 to 15). A recommendation for additional treatment, called 'adjuvant therapy' (Chapter 23) is based on weighing the likelihood that your cancer will grow back after the surgery against the unnecessary side effects caused by too much treatment.

If the risk of regrowth in the 'local area' (breast or chest wall and lymph nodes) is substantial, then adjuvant radiation therapy is used (Chapter 25). Except for women in the 'lowest risk' category of possible recurrence, additional therapy aimed at the entire body will also be offered (tamoxifen, other hormone therapy or chemotherapy; Chapters 28 and 30). If recurrence in the local area and throughout the rest of the body are both a concern, combined types of adjuvant therapy may be recommended, for example, radiation plus chemotherapy.

The Surgical Options

CHAPTER SEVENTEEN

Staging and prognosis

What is staging?

AFTER THE DIAGNOSIS OF CANCER has been made it is important
to determine the extent or 'stage' of the cancer before deciding
on the treatment plan. Briefly, cancer that is small and confined
to the breast is at an early stage, whereas one that has spread to
other parts of the body is advanced or metastatic. Based on a
detailed knowledge of the extent of the disease, your surgeon or
oncologist (cancer specialist) can make recommendations about
the chances of being cured by surgery alone, type of surgery that
is likely to give you the best possible outcome, and whether
additional treatments (radiation, hormone or chemotherapy)
will be helpful.

The physical examination

One of the most important investigations is the physical
examination done by the surgeon or oncologist. Your lungs,
liver, abdomen, back and limbs will be examined for abnormalities. Your breast will be examined and any lumps will be measured. Your armpit and neck will be felt to see if any lymph

nodes are enlarged. Not all enlarged lymph nodes are cancerous: the doctor will try to determine this by assessing whether a node feels normal or enlarged, soft or hard, and whether it is movable. If a suspicious lymph node is found, a fine-needle aspiration is done (see Chapter 11). Unfortunately, simple physical examination of the armpit is not foolproof, and sometimes cancerous lymph nodes are not found until surgery.

Blood tests

Blood tests will be done to check whether your bone marrow, liver and kidneys are working normally. Some surgeons also order blood tests to look for 'tumor markers,' which are proteins that leak out of cancer cells and can be measured in the blood. Although these markers are not reliable for diagnosing cancer, they can be useful for checking the response to treatment, especially in cases of metastatic cancer. The tumor markers usually measured in breast cancer are CEA (carcino-embryonic antigen) and CA 15-3.

Other tests

Most surgeons also order a chest x-ray to check the condition of the lungs and to check for any benign or malignant lung disease. For older women, an electrocardiogram (ECG) may be done to check the heart.

A bone scan is only necessary for women who have a high risk of metastasis to the bones or actual symptoms of such metastases. For example, a bone scan would be done before surgery if the cancer lump is larger than 5 cm or if there are enlarged lymph nodes in the armpit. The same goes for ultra-sound examinations of the liver. If liver metastases are highly unlikely then an ultrasound is not done routinely.

Official systems of staging

There are several systems for classifying the extent or stage of breast cancer. The two most common are the Stage I, II, III, IV system (Table 6) and the TNM system (Table 7).

Table 6 **Stage definitions (I to IV) of breast cancer**	
Definition	Average five-year survival
STAGE I	
Tumor less than 2 cm, no metastases, no cancer in lymph nodes	80% to 95%
STAGE II	
Tumor 2-5 cm but not involving skin and chest wall. If lymph nodes are involved they must be movable	50% to 70%
STAGE III	
Advanced local tumor, fixed to the skin or chest wall, or presence of lymph nodes 'attached' to structures in the axilla	30% to 60%
STAGE IV	
Cancer spread beyond the breast and axilla, to lymph nodes above the collarbone, or to distant organs	5% to 20%

One very important point to realize about these staging systems is that they provide just rough estimates of the stage of disease and chances of survival. The numbers are just averages. They do not say anything about the outcome or prognosis of any one particular woman. Each case is unique and other details of your own case, not just the size and location of tumor, are used to help determine your chance of being cured by surgery alone or with additional therapy. In other words, these staging systems, although important, are used simply to provide an approximate idea of the extent of disease to help plan the treatment strategy, but they are far too basic to precisely determine an individual woman's outcome.

The Stage I, II, III, IV system

This simple system defines four stages of breast cancer (see Table 6). Stage I represents early cancer, with a small tumor and

Table 7 **The TNM staging system**

TUMOR Stages: (T)

T(0):   no identifiable tumor in the breast
Tis: in situ (noninvasive) cancer only
T(1):   invasive cancer 2 cm or less in diameter
T(2):   invasive cancer 2 cm to 5 cm in diameter
T(3):   invasive cancer larger than 5 cm without skin
        or chest wall involvement
T(4a): tumor of any size fixed to the chest wall
T(4b): tumor of any size invading the skin
T(4c): tumor of any size invading both chest wall and the skin
T(4d): inflammatory cancer

NODE Stages: (N)

N(0):   no evidence of palpable lymph nodes
N(1):   palpable, mobile lymph nodes in the armpit only
N(2):   lymph nodes in the axilla are fixed to each other or to
        adjacent structures such as nerves, muscles, skin or bones
N(3):   involved lymph nodes beside the breast bone

METASTASIS Stages: (M)

M(0):   no evidence of metastases
M(1):   metastases present including spread to lymph nodes
        above the collarbone

no spread to the lymph nodes in the armpit. In stages II and III, the tumor is progressively more advanced, while stage IV refers to metastatic disease that has spread to other areas of the body.

Since each stage (I to IV) is rather broad, the survival expectation within each stage is quite variable. For example, for a woman with stage I cancer the average survival at five years after diagnosis is 85%. However, within this category there could be a woman with a mammographically detected cancer of just 0.5 cm in diameter as well as another woman with a 2 cm diameter tumor and cancer invading the lymphatic vessels in the breast. The first woman would have a 95% chance of living free of cancer for over 10 years while the second woman would have a survival expectation closer to that of women with stage II tumors (a 30% to 50% chance of recurrence within five years).

Also, keep in mind that the five-year survival rates in Table 6 are only estimates and your individual chance may be quite different.

The TNM system

The TNM system defines the extent of the cancer based on three features of the tumor: the size/extent of the tumor (T), lymph node involvement (N), and the presence or absence of metastases (M). There are nine possible 'T' categories, four 'N' categories, and two 'M' categories. This system is not as simple as the Stage I, II, III, IV system for everyday use but it is useful for cancer specialists to communicate with each other.

CHAPTER EIGHTEEN

The doctor has suggested surgery: What should I do?

THE OPERATIONS OF TODAY are much less extensive than they used to be. When it comes to surgery, 'more' is not necessarily 'better.' These days there is usually a team of experts who treat the cancer by a combination of surgery, radiation, chemotherapy and hormones. You are also part of the team and have a role to play — learning about the disease, hearing the options, discussing your needs with your family and friends, and coming to a comfortable decision about what you want.

Although long delays are not advised, you should not be rushed or pushed into accepting a treatment plan before you are ready, even if it means requesting a second opinion or waiting a week or so for surgery. You should feel informed and confident.

Do I need surgery?

Having heard of chemotherapy and radiation, many women question the need for surgery, but for most breast cancers, surgery is advisable for a number of good reasons. Some women may be completely cured by surgery alone. For others, surgical removal of the tumor provides better control of the cancer in the breast than radiation therapy alone. In addition, the tissues obtained during surgery provide important information about the type of cancer, size, extent of lymph node involvement and the level of estrogen receptors (see Chapter 30). This information allows the oncologist to determine the stage of the cancer and to tailor any further treatment to your particular case. For instance, if a very tiny cancer is found during surgery, only radiation may be needed to complete the treatment, but if the cancer is more extensive, chemotherapy may also be recommended.

For some cancers, surgery is not the best treatment to start with. This is the case if the tumor is 'locally advanced,' meaning that there is either a very large breast lump or very enlarged lymph nodes, or it is the inflammatory type of cancer. In these situations chemotherapy and radiation may be given first to reduce the size of the tumor. Afterwards, mastectomy may be recommended to remove the primary tumor and reduce the risk of cancer recurrence in the breast.

In the rare instance when there is evidence that the cancer has already spread beyond both the breast and axillary lymph nodes, the initial treatment may include hormones, chemotherapy and radiation, rather than surgery. In this situation, the cancer that has already spread outside the breast is the greater threat, and must be treated first rather than focusing on the breast itself.

Choosing a surgeon

How can you find the best surgeon for you? Usually, one surgeon cannot be singled out who is best for everyone in all circumstances. The ideal surgeon is knowledgeable about breast surgery and current practices as well as being skilful in the operating room. Your surgeon should be someone with whom you feel confident. Don't be uncomfortable about requesting a second opinion if you want one.

Most patients leave the choice of surgeon to their family doctor. This is fine provided you have confidence in both your family doctor and his or her choice. However, you should be aware that family practitioners may not be in a position to refer you to the best surgeon for your case because of standardized referral habits that they use or because they work in a restrictive group practice. Also, remember that your doctor knows the surgeon as a colleague and not as a patient. If you have a good relationship with your doctor or have already discussed your cancer with an oncologist, you may simply need a surgeon who has good surgical technique.

Recommendations by friends tend to be based on the quality of the surgeon's bedside manner. Good information about surgeons can be obtained from women volunteering with the Reach-to-Recovery program of the Cancer Society or other local support and advocacy groups for breast cancer. The women in support groups will have opinions based on their personal experiences and they will share them with you. You must keep in mind that the best surgeons do not necessarily possess the warmest bedside manner. You should, however, be able to ask the surgeon questions and get satisfactory answers.

Many local cancer clinics have 'breast cancer policy groups.' Surgeons participating in such a group will be aware of current trends and practices and may be more able to respond to your questions.

CHAPTER NINETEEN

Types of breast surgery

Why are there so many choices?

THERE ARE MANY TYPES OF SURGERY available for the treatment of breast cancer. Why isn't there just one operation? Each procedure has its advantages and disadvantages, depending on the situation. The type of operation best for you depends on a combination of factors: the type of cancer, its size and location, your preference, the surgeon's preference, and the policies of the hospital or cancer center where the treatment takes place.

Take time to consider your options

While it is true that you shouldn't delay surgery too long, most cancers have been present for a number of years and there is no need to rush into the operating room by nightfall. A delay of one to two weeks is usually less important than careful consideration of the surgical options. You should understand your choices and feel comfortable with them. There is time for a well thought out choice based on careful examination of the options, discussions with other patients, a second opinion if desired, and an evaluation of your needs with your family and supporters.

Don't assume that you can't understand the various details of the treatment and give up control because of feelings of anxiety or fear. Spend a few days talking with others and thinking about which route is best for you. Taking this time to decide what you want leads to an informed choice that ensures that you remain confident and have some measure of control. In the long run, this is time well spent.

Operations that save the breast

Lumpectomy (tumorectomy)

Strictly speaking, a lumpectomy refers to the operation in which only the lump that is obvious to the naked eye is removed, leaving the rest of the breast tissue alone. However, it is not always possible to see how extensive the lump actually is, so it is difficult to know if removing the lump has removed all of the cancer. Tiny, microscopic 'tentacles' of cancer cells, which cannot be felt by the surgeon, often grow out from the edge of the lump. Since leaving in these tentacles of cancer cells leads to a greater chance of the cancer recurring in the breast, it is recommended that some normal breast tissue around the tumor be removed with the tumor itself, as described in the partial mastectomy (below). A partial mastectomy is often also referred to as a lumpectomy, so it is important to ask physicians to clarify the type of operation they are referring to.

Partial mastectomy: removing a small amount of the breast

A partial mastectomy (also known as 'lumpectomy,' 'segmental mastectomy' or 'wide excision') is an operation that removes some normal breast tissue surrounding the cancer (Figure 24). (In this book we will use the term 'partial mastectomy.') This has become the most commonly performed surgery for the treatment of breast cancer. Studies have found that a partial mastectomy followed by radiation gives a woman the same chance of survival and control of the local cancer as does a modified radical mastectomy (an operation that removes the breast, discussed further on). The fear of the cancer returning should not be the reason for choosing one type of surgery over the other.

Figure 24: A partial mastectomy involves removing some normal breast tissue surrounding the cancer. The axillary dissection is performed through a separate incision in the armpit.

When the cancer and breast tissue is taken out, careful attention is paid to the edges of the tissue being removed to make certain that they don't contain any cancer. The idea is to remove the cancer lump together with any of its 'tentacles' that extend into the normal breast tissue, but still leave enough tissue that the breast looks 'normal.'

There are several types of partial mastectomies. In the 'wide excision' of a lump, more normal breast tissue is taken than in a lumpectomy. A 'quadrantectomy' involves the removal of a quarter of the breast and skin. The result of a skilfully done partial mastectomy should look very comparable to the appearance of the untreated breast (Figure 25). The area that is cut depends partly on the location of the tumor, the size of the breast, and the surgeon's preference. The goal of the surgery is to remove the cancer but leave the breast as normal-appearing as possible.

Partial mastectomy combined with axillary dissection (removal of lymph nodes in the armpit)

Along with removing the actual tumor from the breast, many surgeons also remove the axillary lymph nodes from the armpit. This is known as an axillary dissection, and may be done at the same time as a partial mastectomy. There are two reasons for doing this. Axillary dissection removes any of the cancer that may have spread to the lymph nodes. Also, by removing the lymph nodes and analyzing them under the microscope, more information is obtained on the stage of the cancer in the nodes, if there is any. This will determine the type of chemotherapy, radiation or hormone therapy that is offered after surgery.

There may be 30 to 50 lymph nodes in the axilla (armpit) but usually, if five to ten nodes are removed this is sufficient to give information about prognosis. It is no longer considered appropriate to do a 'clean-out' since this does not improve survival

Figure 25: Five years after a partial mastectomy and radiotherapy for a cancer of the right breast.

and does increase the chance of complications such as arm swelling and pain.

An axillary dissection is usually done under general anesthetic and may require a few days in hospital. A separate incision is made in the armpit (Figure 24). Just before closing the wound, the surgeon places a small tube, called a 'drain,' into the area where the lymph nodes were, to collect fluid that would otherwise accumulate. The other end of the tube comes out through the surface of the skin and is sewn to the skin to keep it in place. In a few days, when less fluid is draining through the tube, the drain is removed.

Operations that remove the breast

Simple (total) mastectomy

A simple mastectomy is the removal of the entire breast without removing any muscles or axillary lymph nodes. This procedure is useful if the entire breast must be removed and there is no suspicion of cancer in the axillary nodes. For example, for a woman who has a strong family history of breast cancer and who decides to have both breasts removed to eliminate the risk of developing breast cancer (not a decision to be taken lightly), a simple mastectomy is the best operation because it removes all of the breast tissue while preserving everything else, including lymph nodes and muscle. Another situation in which a simple mastectomy could be done is for a widespread ductal carcinoma in situ. A true simple mastectomy will include removal of some skin and the nipple.

Subcutaneous mastectomy

As with the simple mastectomy, this operation has been used to prevent future cancer in a woman at high risk. In a subcutaneous mastectomy, the breast tissue is 'dug out' through a small incision while preserving the breast, skin and nipple. The main disadvantage of this operation is that approximately 15% of the breast tissue is left behind. Therefore it is an unsuitable operation for complete cancer prevention. In addition, results of reconstructive surgery may not be quite as good after a subcutaneous mastectomy.

Figure 26: Extent of tissue removed (A) and appearance after a modified radical mastectomy (B).

Modified radical mastectomy

Modified radical mastectomy was the standard surgical procedure for breast cancer for many years. It involves the total removal of the breast along with the axillary lymph nodes, some skin and the nipple (Figure 26). It is called 'modified' because it removes fewer surrounding muscles and lymph nodes than the original radical mastectomy that is now rarely done (see below). A modified radical mastectomy does not remove the chest wall muscles or nerves. This technique is suitable for most patients with stage I or II breast cancer who are not interested in conserving their breasts.

An incision is made over the breast, and the resulting scar after removal of the breast and lymph nodes is long and straight or diagonal across the chest wall (Figure 26). Ask your surgeon how the scar will look and what measures he or she can take to make it easier for you to consider reconstructive surgery if you decide to have it later. A modified radical mastectomy is usually done under general anesthetic and requires a hospital stay of between two to seven days. As the armpit lymph nodes are removed, a drain tube is left in place to avoid fluid build-up.

Radical mastectomy

Radical mastectomy includes removal of the breast, the *pectoralis major* and *minor* chest wall muscles, some nerves, the nipple, the skin, and all of the lymph nodes in the armpit right up to the collarbone. The incision goes all the way from the armpit down to the top of the abdomen. The chest wall ends up looking deformed due to the loss of muscle. Because so much tissue is removed a skin graft is usually needed.

Although these days a radical mastectomy should rarely be necessary, there are cases in which a toned-down version of it might occasionally be considered. An example is a large tumor that has invaded the chest wall muscles so that the only way to remove it completely is by removing a portion of the chest muscle as well as the breast and skin.

CHAPTER TWENTY

Treatment of
in situ breast cancer

Treatment of ductal carcinoma in situ

DUCTAL CARCINOMA IN SITU refers to breast cancer that is still entirely within the milk ducts of the breast and has not invaded nearby tissues. Therefore, it has not had any chance to spread to other parts of the body. Chapter 14 provides a description of this type of cancer.

Breast conservation is an option

In the past, the traditional treatment for ductal carcinoma in situ was a simple (total) mastectomy to prevent the progression to invasive cancer. Although the cure rate after such a mastectomy is 95% to 99%, many women are interested in a treatment that conserves the breast and still provides an excellent chance of a cure. Studies have now shown that partial mastectomy followed by radiation therapy is effective and is a common choice of treatment. The procedure for partial mastectomy is discussed in Chapter 19.

To remove the entire ductal carcinoma in situ and conserve the breast it is critical that the surgeon plan the operation with a clear idea of the mammogram appearance of the cancer. As well, the pathologist must inspect many samples of the removed tissue to ensure that no invasive cancer is present, and to give an estimate of the completeness of the excision.

In most cases, if the in situ cancer appears to have been completely removed and radiation therapy is given, it is possible to save the breast. A woman who chooses the breast conservation approach requires lifelong follow-up so that if recurrence develops she can receive treatment at a stage when a cure is still possible. About half of these recurrences will be invasive cancers and the rest will be more in situ ductal carcinomas. Usually, if the recurrence occurs after excision and radiation therapy for the initial cancer, then a mastectomy is necessary.

If the ductal carcinoma in situ is extensive

If the in situ cancer is widespread (more than 5 cm across), the amount of tissue that must be removed often leads to unacceptable disfigurement of the breast. Also, even after radiation therapy there may be a high (30% to 40%) chance of recurrence in the breast. Since about half of these recurrences will be invasive cancers with the possibility of distant spread, simple mastectomy and reconstruction is often recommended when the in situ cancer is very extensive to maximize the chances of a long-term cure.

Wide excision (partial mastectomy) alone for very small ductal carcinomas in situ

For some women with very small areas of ductal carcinoma in situ it may be possible to save the breast and avoid radiation therapy. For this procedure to be successful, the cancer should measure less than 1 cm in diameter on both the mammogram and in the pathology specimen, AND the area must be removed along with a wide margin of normal tissue.

Comedocarcinoma

'Comedocarcinoma' is a sub-type of ductal carcinoma in situ that tends to develop recurrences more often than the other types of in situ cancer and also tends to form invasive cancers earlier. To achieve the best control, most authorities recommend adding radiation after wide excision for any size of comedocarcinoma, even if it is very small.

The box below summarizes current recommendations for the management of ductal carcinoma in situ.

Options for the treatment of ductal carcinoma in situ

Wide excision (partial mastectomy) alone is appropriate if:

- The cancer is less than 1 cm AND
- Non-comedocarcinoma subtype AND
- Normal breast tissue was seen between the cancer and the marked margins by the pathologist

Wide excision (partial mastectomy) plus radiation therapy is appropriate if:

- The cancer is 1 to 5 cm in diameter OR
- Was the comedocarcinoma subtype OR
- The marked margin was close to cancerous tissue as seen by the pathologist

Simple (total) mastectomy is appropriate if:

- The cancer is extensive (more than 5 cm in diameter of calcifications on mammogram) OR
- The margins still show cancer after two attempts at wide excision OR
- The patient chooses this option for any size or type of in situ cancer

---

Tamoxifen is still being studied

Current research is evaluating the use of the anti-estrogen drug tamoxifen in the treatment of ductal carcinoma in situ to determine whether it may reduce the chances of recurrence or invasion. However, as of 1996 there is no proven role for tamoxifen alone in the management of pure in situ cancer.

Treatment of lobular carcinoma in situ

Women with lobular carcinoma in situ (also called lobular neoplasia) have a high risk of developing an invasive breast cancer, more so than with ductal carcinoma in situ. These invasive cancers are about as likely to develop in either breast, so any therapy has to be directed at both breasts.

One course of action is to undertake careful, regular screening and follow-up. Another, drastic choice that has been used is preventive removal of both breasts (bilateral 'prophylactic' mastectomy; see Chapter 19 on 'simple mastectomy'). This is done very occasionally if a woman's fear of developing breast cancer outweighs her desire to save her breasts. This surgery may be recommended if there is a family history of breast cancer in addition to lobular carcinoma in situ.

Lobular cancers are almost always estrogen receptor-positive (see Chapter 30), which suggests that the anti-estrogen drug tamoxifen might be able to 'block' the stimulating effect of natural estrogens and help prevent the development of invasive cancers. A large study is now in progress to test tamoxifen's effectiveness in this and other high-risk situations. Although tamoxifen is usually well tolerated, it does have some potentially serious side effects, so women are not advised to take tamoxifen 'routinely' until it can be demonstrated that tamoxifen is effective for preventing the development of invasive breast cancer in women with lobular carcinoma in situ and tolerable to these otherwise healthy individuals.

What type of surgery
is best for me?

Does one type of surgery offer a better chance of cure?

THE AIM OF SURGERY is to give you the best chance of being cured of the cancer. Usually, the choice is between a partial mastectomy or a modified radical mastectomy (explained in Chapter 19). Studies show that partial mastectomy followed by radiation or modified radical mastectomy without radiation provide an equal chance of cure and a high chance (85% to 92%) of controlling the cancer in the breast or chest wall. Therefore, your choice of one operation or the other need NOT be based on the 'relapse rate.'

How do I choose the right surgery?

A partial mastectomy is suitable for about 75% of patients. Usually a woman will feel better about herself if she can keep her breast, but there are a number of other factors you and your surgeon should consider:

a) Your preference
b) The surgical issues, including the size of the breast, size of the tumor, its location and the type of cancer cells

c) Your age and general health
d) Your ability to undergo radiation
e) Your availability for regular follow-up visits after the surgery is done.

Your preference counts

Whenever possible, YOUR PREFERENCE should be the deciding factor. A modified radical mastectomy may seem like the better solution for a woman whose breasts are difficult to examine and is 'never going to trust that breast again.' On the other hand, a partial mastectomy conserves the breast and avoids the discomfort and necessity of wearing an artificial breast (prosthesis). Studies have shown that one year after surgery women have similar levels of distress regardless of whether they have had their breast removed or saved. In other words, the diagnosis of cancer causes anxiety no matter what type of surgery is done. Other studies have shown that women who are GIVEN THE CHOICE of surgical treatment adjust to the diagnosis of breast cancer more easily than women who are told to have a particular type of operation.

Surgical issues

Surgical considerations include the size and location of the tumor compared to the size of the breast. If the tumor is large and the breast small, a partial mastectomy may remove too much breast tissue, leaving a disappointing cosmetic result. In this case a modified radical mastectomy may be preferable, with the option of breast reconstruction either later or at the same time. As a rule, tumors smaller than 3 cm can almost always be removed by a partial mastectomy, tumors larger than 5 cm are removed by modified radical mastectomy, and the size of the breast must be carefully considered for tumors between 3 and 5 cm. (If the tumor is very large, your surgeon may suggest that chemotherapy and radiation be given before surgery.)

The location of the tumor can also affect the cosmetic result of a partial mastectomy. If it's in the centre of the breast the nipple may have to be removed, resulting in a less satisfactory appearance as well as loss of nipple sensation. If the partial mastectomy is done well, however, the result may be superior to a modified radical mastectomy and reconstruction, or mastectomy and a prosthesis.

About 1% of women are found to have two or more tumors in one breast. If there are multiple tumors within the breast it may not be possible to remove all the affected areas without doing a modified radical mastectomy. Multiple tumors are usually identified before surgery on the mammograms, but sometimes this situation is only identified in the pathology report after surgery.

Your overall health affects your ability to undergo radiation

The state of your general health is an important factor when deciding if a partial mastectomy is the best treatment for you. Since radiation is generally required with a partial mastectomy to reduce the risk of recurrence, this type of operation should not be recommended if you are not suitable for radiation. Radiation treatment may be difficult for someone who is elderly or very weak and has difficulty visiting a clinic every day for up to six weeks. Patients who cannot lie flat on the treatment table, or who cannot lift their arms over their head for the radiation treatment (for example after a stroke) will have difficulty with this part of the treatment. Therefore, they may be advised to have a modified radical mastectomy instead.

You would also be considered unsuitable for radiation treatment if it is felt that you have a high risk of severe side effects (see Chapter 26). Some women who have certain other medical conditions should not receive radiation if they have a choice. These conditions include severe lung disease, including previous tuberculosis, or severe heart disease. Women with systemic lupus erythematosus (SLE), scleroderma or ataxia-telangiectasia may have severe reactions and scarring from the radiation so they may best be treated by a modified radical mastectomy. Women who are pregnant should also avoid radiation if possible because it may damage the fetus.

Women with very large breasts tend to get more radiation side effects because of the large amount of tissue that must be treated. Also, radiation should not be given to a woman who has already received radiation therapy to her breast sometime in the past.

Partial mastectomy means regular follow-up visits

After a partial mastectomy and radiation the breast should be observed regularly and carefully to detect early, potentially curable cancer that may recur. You should get to know the 'normal feel' of your treated breast. After surgery and radiation there are often areas of thickening or lumpiness. This is normal but changes in the lumpiness should be reported to your doctor. The best way to monitor your breasts is by a monthly breast self-examination. You should also have a physical examination every six months by a knowledgeable physician, for example your surgeon, an oncologist, or another experienced physician. We also recommend a mammogram six months after the radiation treatment is completed, followed by mammograms of both breasts at least annually. It is important that women who opt for breast-saving therapy such as partial mastectomy realize that they must be available for this close follow-up. If, for geographic or other reasons, follow-up is not possible, a modified radical mastectomy may be a safer option.

Is a partial mastectomy better than a modified radical mastectomy?

It is important to understand that in most cases, a breast-saving operation such as a partial mastectomy followed by radiation is as good as a modified radical mastectomy. This doesn't mean that a partial mastectomy is better, but it does allow you to make a choice. You should consider the risks and benefits of both, and your doctors should give you sufficient information and the respect to allow you to make an informed choice.

The advantage of a breast-saving operation is that there is no amputation. This must be weighed against the need for a series of radiation treatments, and a more careful and prolonged follow-up. The advantage of a modified radical mastectomy is that the treatment is over at once, avoiding radiation treatments. If there is a large cancer or more than one cancer in the affected breast, or if certain conditions make radiation more hazardous, mastectomy may be the better option. However, it does mean that a part of you would be amputated. No one answer is always 'right': each person is different. Therefore, it is appropriate and healthy for you to participate in this important decision.

CHAPTER TWENTY-TWO

Hospitalization and recovering from surgery

The recovery room

IN THE RECOVERY ROOM nurses carefully monitor you as you wake up. Often, patients are confused for a short period. Also, you may have a sore throat after a breast operation. This is a temporary discomfort from the breathing tube that was inserted in your mouth and down your throat during the operation. The doctor has provided a list of orders, including pain relief and other medications.

Your surgeon may come to talk to you here, although you may be too groggy to remember much. Only a few preliminary findings will be known right away, as the full pathology report is usually not available for three to five days.

Notifying your significant other

There is usually someone you will want the surgeon to contact when the operation is finished, so that person's name and phone number should be clearly written in your chart. If your significant other is waiting in the hospital, make sure it is clear exactly where they are since the surgeon may want to talk to them while you are in the recovery room to describe what was found.

The ward

The type of operation and your recovery time will determine how long you stay in hospital. Most patients go home two to three days after a partial mastectomy and within five days after a modified radical mastectomy. The sooner patients start moving around after surgery the fewer problems they have, so you will be urged to get out of bed and walk up and down the halls.

Pain

After the surgery there will be some pain that can be controlled with pain killers. Everyone is different, so it is important for you to let the nurse know when you are in pain so you can receive medication according to your needs. Some patients feel nauseated after an anesthetic while others may have shivers when they wake up. As well, many of the pain killers can cause nausea and constipation but this is usually mild and temporary.

Drains

If you have an axillary dissection or a modified radical mastectomy, you may have one or two drains in the area for the first few days to avoid fluid accumulating. The drains are removed before you leave hospital or a few days later, depending on the amount of fluid and how long you stay in hospital. Sometimes after the drain is removed the fluid builds up again and needs to be removed with a syringe. This can be done easily in the surgeon's office during an outpatient visit.

Sutures

Some stitches (sutures) may eventually dissolve on their own while other non-absorbable sutures or staples need to be removed, usually a week to ten days after the surgery. Ask your surgeon what sort of sutures will be used. The redness of your scar will gradually fade over several months.

A note about visitors

A stay in hospital tends to bring friends and relatives out of the woodwork. Depending on your personality, this may or may not please you. If it doesn't, the simplest way of avoiding the stress of attending a steady stream of visitors is not to announce to anyone other than your immediate family that you are having surgery. The ward clerk can also put up a sign restricting visitors.

It may be that seeing people and discussing the situation will be helpful, especially with people close to you who are supportive. Make sure, however, that the visitors do not need more support than you do, and that you do not let the socializing wear you out.

Going home: ask questions before you leave

You are bound to have questions about what you can do when you get home, so write them down and be prepared to rattle off the list when you see your doctor for the last time in hospital. Make sure you understand what you can and cannot do, what exercises you should do to start moving your arm and when you should start them, when you should see the surgeon again and when you may see an oncologist. Also, make sure you have a prescription for pain killers because you may need them, especially as you get more active.

Dealing with hospitalization

You may find the hospital's admission routine a source of frustration. You may feel that you are answering the same questions over and over again, but nobody seems to be listening. Hospital procedures require that a patient be admitted by the clerk, the ward nurse, and a number of doctors, including the surgeon and anesthetist. In a teaching hospital the list may also include a student nurse, a medical student, an intern and a resident. Be patient: they are listening, but each of them requires slightly different information. The many questions are useful to ensure that any allergies you suffer are recorded as well as the list of any medication you take regularly, and that everyone knows you individually.

Surgical residents

Many hospitals are affiliated with universities and have a responsibility to train future practitioners. A strong surgical training program employs residents to give quality care before, during and after surgery. In a teaching hospital the surgical residents participate in an operation not only because it is part of their training, but also because most operations require two sets of hands. While patients accept that their busy surgeons require the assistance of the residents on the ward, they become anxious when they learn that the residents may be participating in and, in some cases, performing their operation. Although many senior surgical residents have as much experience and skill as your surgeon and may provide superior results, it is your right to expect close supervision of the residents by the staff surgeon. Therefore, it is more appropriate to ask, 'Who is directing the operation?' rather than, 'Who is doing the operation?' A major operation is a team effort in which residents play an important role.

Possible problems and discomfort later on

Most women do suffer some pain, initially along the incision and under the arm. It may last a few days to a few weeks or longer and can be controlled with pain medications. Later on, some women complain of a tightness or discomfort over the chest area which, although mild, is often bothersome and longer-lasting. This is usually helped by physiotherapy (see Chapter 33). The incision usually heals within a few weeks, but may take somewhat longer in women who have had radiation before surgery.

The risk of infection with breast surgery is usually low, but if there is a foul-smelling drainage, increasingly red and tender skin or any fever, there may be an infection and it should be treated promptly with antibiotics.

If the lymph nodes are removed from the armpit there will be some disruption of the normal lymph drainage. Any later infection in your hand or arm will increase the risk of complications such as permanent arm swelling. Radiation treatment to the armpit may also worsen these problems. You can take a number of precautionary steps to avoid significant arm edema (swelling) and the related pain and discomfort that can occur (see Chapter 33).

After breast surgery many women complain about numbness in the back of the underarm or on the chest wall. This is usually due to nerves being cut or stretched during the operation, and may improve in the months ahead.

Breast surgery is emotionally difficult for many women. Often, it is difficult for a patient to look at her own body, let alone show her spouse, friends or family the scars. As the incision fades and you use your arm, you can begin to heal. A breast cancer support group and a physiotherapy consultation is often helpful to regain your sense of your body.

Obtaining a breast prosthesis

If you have been treated with a mastectomy you may want to consider a prosthesis or breast reconstruction (see Chapter 34). The prosthesis is a soft, somewhat heavy plastic form that comes in many shapes and sizes to match the many shapes and sizes of women's breasts (Figure 27).

Reach-to-Recovery volunteers who work with the Cancer Society will often supply a soft, 'fluffy' breast form of cotton that you can wear temporarily in your own bra. This helps fill out your clothes but does not have the weight or shape of your other breast. A fitted prosthesis will help you feel better and walk straighter. Once the initial pain and swelling of the mastectomy has settled and the wound is healed you are ready for a 'fitting.' This is often four to six weeks after surgery. However, some women wait longer since it is important to be psychologically 'ready' for the prosthesis for a successful fitting.

What to look for

Breast prostheses are not one-size-fits-all and just picking a form off the shelf will not give you the best fit. You need to consider the size, shape and weight of your remaining breast to get a good match. The traditional prosthesis is sold with a specially designed bra with a pocket into which the prosthesis can fit. A recent innovation is a prosthesis which directly adheres to the chest wall. It is attached to the chest by strips of velcro which are glued to the chest and the underside of the prosthesis. Body heat activates the adhesive properties of the glue and the velcro strips remain on the chest wall for a week to 10 days. They come off without the tearing or 'ouch' of the usual adhesive plasters.

Additional garments are available such as bathing suits and nightgowns that are specially designed to hold the prosthesis.

Where to get your prosthesis

Depending on where you live there may be many or just a few places to buy a prosthesis such as department or drug stores. In larger towns you can find stores that specialize in selling and fitting prostheses and garments to wear with the prothesis. When selecting your retailer, expect the salesperson to offer empathy and sensitivity, but also expect that she has completed training courses in fitting prostheses and that she is aware of the full range of products available today. Your surgeon, Reach-to-Recovery volunteer, local Cancer Society office or nurses at your regional cancer treatment center should be able to direct you to a store. Breast prostheses are a medical appliance so you should check if the cost will be covered by your medical insurance.

Figure 27: A plastic breast prosthesis in a customized bra.

Preventing Recurrence of Cancer

CHAPTER TWENTY-THREE

Additional treatment following surgery: Radiation, chemotherapy and hormone treatment

Why is additional treatment needed?

EVEN WHEN THE CANCER appears to have been totally removed, the surgeon can never be sure that he or she 'got it all.' This is because microscopic cells may have been left behind, or they may have spread elsewhere in the body as tiny, undetectable metastases. This is a frustrating problem because only 'time will tell' whether or not the operation was indeed a cure. Until then, the surgery must be considered as 'potentially curative.'

Therefore, treatment is given IN ADDITION to surgery, as a preventive measure, in case cancer is still present. This preventive treatment is called 'adjuvant' therapy. The choices include radiation therapy, chemotherapy, and hormonal agents.

Who should receive adjuvant therapy?

Because we are not able to detect the presence of just a few microscopic cancer cells, each patient's risk of cancer recurrence is assessed based on the surgical findings and the pathology report (see Table 4, Chapter 13).

Based on this assessment, adjuvant therapy may or may not be recommended to a particular patient. For instance, a woman with a very low risk of cancer recurrence and a high probability (more than 90%) of being cured by surgery alone may not be offered any adjuvant therapy. New recommendations are constantly being developed to keep pace with the ever improving understanding of breast cancer.

When should adjuvant therapy start?

Adjuvant therapy is usually started within four to eight weeks after surgery. It is sometimes difficult for women to accept the need for additional treatment so soon after surgery, especially because it requires one to admit the possibility of the cancer returning. Ideally, the concept of adjuvant therapy is best discussed before surgery to give women more time to consider it and come to terms with the reasons for it.

Types of adjuvant therapy

Radiotherapy

Adjuvant radiotherapy is given after partial mastectomy. Although the cancer may seem to have been removed completely, the likelihood of the cancer coming back in the same breast is relatively high (up to 40% over 10 years without radiation). Radiation to the breast can significantly reduce these recurrences.

Women who have had a modified radical mastectomy may also be treated by adjuvant radiation if the tumor is large (more than 5 cm), if it is invading the skin or the chest wall, or if multiple lymph nodes are cancerous. In this situation, adjuvant radiation decreases the chance of the cancer recurring on the chest wall or in the lymph node areas (see Chapter 25).

Chemotherapy

Adjuvant chemotherapy is given after surgery when there is a risk of residual cancer cells regrowing as metastases throughout the body. Adjuvant chemotherapy decreases the risk of this recurrence and increases the number of women cured. In chemotherapy, drugs are given by mouth, or more often, directly into the vein (see Chapters 27 to 29).

Hormone therapy

Like chemotherapy, hormone therapy is also effective against breast cancer cells that may have 'escaped.' The most common form of hormone therapy is a drug called tamoxifen that blocks the effect of the hormone, estrogen, in the body. The connection between estrogen and cancer growth is discussed in Chapter 30. Postmenopausal women appear to benefit from tamoxifen but its use in premenopausal women is still being studied.

Other types of hormonal therapies exist, including reducing the estrogen levels of premenopausal women by surgical removal of the ovaries. Radiation to the ovaries can achieve the same effect and is also sometimes used as adjuvant treatment.

Combined adjuvant therapy

Depending on the type of surgery and the extent of the cancer when it is discovered, more than one type of adjuvant therapy may be offered. Each woman's situation is different. Therefore, one woman may receive both radiotherapy and hormone therapy following her surgery, while another may get chemotherapy alone. When more than one type of adjuvant therapy is used it is called 'combined modality treatment.'

Radiation Therapy

Radiation therapy: what is it?

How does radiation work?

RADIATION THERAPY, also called 'radiotherapy,' is the use of high-energy rays to kill cancer cells. Radiation works by damaging the cells so that they eventually die. Radiation will damage any type of cell, either normal or cancerous, that lies in the path of the beam. Therefore, great care must be taken to aim the beam only at the required part of the body and avoid treatment of healthy tissue as much as possible.

Fortunately, normal cells repair themselves from radiation damage more completely than cancer cells do. So, by giving the radiation in a series of small treatments, usually once a day, this lets the normal cells recover between treatments while the cancer cells die.

When is radiation given?

Radiation therapy is used to help prevent recurrence or progression of cancer in one specific part of the body, for example the breast, chest wall or lymph nodes. After a lumpectomy, radiation is directed to the breast to kill any possible 'leftover' cancer cells. It may also be used to treat metastatic cancer in a particular place in the body. For instance, if breast cancer has spread to a woman's hip bone and causes pain, radiation to the hip will kill the cancer cells there and relieve the pain.

The benefits and side effects of radiation therapy are generally restricted to the area being treated. In contrast, chemotherapy agents and hormones are absorbed into the blood stream and affect many parts of the body.

The procedure for getting radiotherapy

The process can be considered in three steps:

a) Deciding whether treatment is advisable
b) A 'planning' visit to the radiation department to mark the area to be treated and to calculate the dose to be used, and
c) The daily visits to receive radiotherapy according to a planned schedule.

The treatment decision

You make the decision to proceed with radiotherapy in consultation with a radiation oncologist (a specialist in radiation therapy). The issues to consider are described in Chapter 25.

The planning session

The purpose of this session is to plan exactly how the x-ray machine is to be directed, given your individual size and body shape, and the location and extent of cancer that requires treatment.

The area to be treated can be marked out by eye or by using a machine called a 'simulator.' The simulator sends low-energy x-rays through the body onto a screen or film so that the target area to be treated can be determined exactly. Very specific information is recorded during the planning session so that the x-ray machine can be accurately re-positioned each time you arrive for a treatment.

Ink marks placed on your body will be used to align the x-ray beam during the daily treatments. It is important not to wash them off until after the treatment is completed. Usually a light dusting of cornstarch will help to keep the skin dry and the marks from rubbing off. A permanent ink dot, the size of a small freckle, is often placed at the center or corner of the treatment area. This 'tattoo' serves as a reference point to avoid mistakenly re-treating an area if radiation is being considered sometime in the future.

Treatment sessions

The amount of radiation you receive and number of daily visits depends on the amount of tissue to be treated, and whether the goal of treatment is to prevent a recurrence or to relieve symptoms. Usually, adjuvant or curative radiation requires anywhere from three and a half to six weeks of daily treatments, and symptom relief requires one to three weeks of treatment.

What happens during radiation treatment?

Radiation treatments are painless. In fact, when the machine is on, the only thing you'll notice is a slight whirring sound. Treatments may be given from several angles each day to make sure that the entire area targeted gets treated.

You will be in the treatment room for about 10 to 20 minutes. Most of this time is spent carefully adjusting the x-ray machine so that it is positioned correctly. During a typical session the machine is turned on for only one to three minutes per treated area each day.

How much radiation is given during radiotherapy?

The radiation dose delivered to the breast is limited by what normal breast tissue can tolerate. The basic unit of radiation dose is called a 'Gray' (1 Gray = 100 rads). The amount of radiation received during a chest x-ray is approximately 0.001 Gray. For a mammogram it is 0.0015 Gray. In contrast, the typical total dose used to treat the whole breast during cancer therapy ranges from 40 Gray (divided into 15 daily doses given over three weeks) up to 50 Gray (divided into 25 daily doses given over five weeks).

Brachytherapy — another way to give radiation

In this procedure, instead of using a machine that sends out an x-ray beam, a tiny piece of radioactive material is implanted directly into a tumor or into the area where the tumor was removed. Radioactive iridium is the substance most often used, but other materials such as radioactive gold and cesium are also employed.

Under general anesthetic, hollow tubes are placed into the area and stitched into place. This is called the 'implant.' Later, on the hospital ward, the doctor or technician places the radioactive iridium into the tubes, either by hand or by a remote-control device. Depending on the radioactive material used and the dose, the radiation sources may be left in place continuously or may be inserted into the implant tubes once or twice a day for several days. During active treatment the hospital room is considered to be radioactive and visitors are restricted.

Can radiation be repeated at some time in the future?

When giving radiotherapy to a part of the body, the idea is to maximize the killing effect on the cancer while staying within safe limits on normal surrounding tissues. So if a part has been given maximum radiation at some time in the past, treatment of that area must not be repeated. Occasionally, if a fairly low dose of radiation was used and cancer regrowth causes symptoms at the same site, the area can be re-treated. Also, if an entirely new area of the body develops problems from cancer, it too can be considered for treatment.

Who benefits
from radiation therapy?

THERE ARE FOUR GENERAL SITUATIONS in which radiotherapy is used for women with breast cancer:

- after breast-saving lumpectomy or partial mastectomy
- after a modified radical mastectomy when there is a high chance of recurrence on the chest wall or in the lymph nodes
- as treatment for locally advanced cancer when surgery is not advisable
- for the relief of symptoms due to cancer recurrence on the chest wall or metastases at other areas such as bones, lymph nodes or the brain.

Radiotherapy following lumpectomy
or partial mastectomy

For most women, the best way to remain free of cancer after breast-conserving surgery is to use radiotherapy after the surgery.

Although it may appear that the entire tumor has been removed, thin 'tentacles' of cancer cells have been known to extend more than ten centimeters from the main tumor. For this reason usually the entire breast is treated with radiation. To avoid unnecessary radiation to the normal structures underneath such as the lung or heart, the radiation is delivered from side to side across the breast (Figure 28).

Radiotherapy after modified radical mastectomy

Modified radical mastectomy (complete removal of the breast) WITHOUT radiotherapy achieves local control of breast cancer for approximately 85% to 90% of patients. However, for some women the risk of cancer regrowth on the chest wall or in the lymph nodes is particularly high, and radiation is recommended even after mastectomy. Radiation may be recommended if the cancer was very large (larger than 5 cm), had invaded the adjacent skin or chest wall muscles, or showed extensive spread to the lymph nodes. In these circumstances radiotherapy can substantially reduce the risk of recurrence on the chest wall or in the lymph nodes but does not change the overall chance of cure.

Radiotherapy for locally extensive cancer

At the time of diagnosis some women already have a cancer that is considered too extensive to treat with surgery, or for some medical reason certain women are considered to be unfit for surgery. These women usually receive chemotherapy or hormone therapy (tamoxifen) depending on their tumor type, age and fitness to withstand treatment. In addition they usually receive radiation to the breast and the nearby lymph nodes. As a result of these treatments, the cancer may shrink to a size that makes surgery possible.

Radiotherapy for recurrence and relief of symptoms from metastases

Radiotherapy can be especially useful to improve the quality of life of patients who have recurrent cancer or who suffer from symptoms caused by cancer that has spread to other areas of the body (metastases). In these situations the radiation works by killing cancer cells, which leads to the cancer lumps shrinking, thereby relieving pain or other symptoms. Pain caused by breast

Figure 28: Woman getting ready for treatment in radiotherapy machine.

cancer metastases in the bones can be relieved in approximately 75% of cases. When there are metastases in the brain, lymph nodes near the breast or some other sites, improvement of symptoms occurs in about 50% of cases.

Unfortunately, radiotherapy is not helpful when the cancer has spread to the lung tissue or the liver because the dose of radiation necessary to kill the cancer cells in these areas is too high for the organs to tolerate. In these situations hormones, chemotherapy or both are used (see Chapter 39).

Side effects of radiation therapy

What radiotherapy does NOT cause

IT IS IMPORTANT TO KNOW that treatments are painless, and, while some people experience nausea, they do not usually vomit, or feel dizzy or lightheaded. You will not lose your hair unless the radiation is specifically directed at your head. Except when brachytherapy is used (a small temporary implant; see Chapter 24), you are NOT radioactive and you are NOT a threat to your friends, family or pets. You should be able to drive yourself back and forth to the clinic for your treatments. Some women even continue full-time employment during radiation treatment.

You may feel tired

Although individuals vary widely in the extent to which they experience side effects, the most common complaint is fatigue. About one woman in three will become noticeably tired. The cause of this is not known, but the best remedy is to have an afternoon nap, maintain a balanced diet, and cut back on stressful activities. After the radiation treatment is finished the fatigue decreases gradually over the next few weeks to months, and it often becomes difficult to tell whether the fatigue is due to the effects of the treatment or the psychological and emotional stress that a new diagnosis of breast cancer brings to every woman.

Emotional effects

Another effect of going to radiation therapy sessions is the daily reminder of the cancer. Many women report feeling weepy, depressed, angry or frustrated. Discuss your feelings with your radiation therapist and oncologist. You will find that it is a normal, common reaction. There may be ways to relieve your sense of frustration by asserting some control over the process by asking questions or helping arrange the timing of your appointments to suit you better.

Side effects in the treated breast

The skin

After a partial mastectomy, the entire breast, skin and chest wall underneath are treated with radiation. During treatment the skin becomes pink, like from a sunburn and sometimes becomes bright red and peels. Afterwards, the skin may appear tanned. Although this tan usually disappears slowly, in about six months to a year, some women are left with slightly darker skin. Occasionally the skin may blister, usually around the nipple or in the crease beneath the breast. Over time the areola on the treated breast may become pale.

It is recommended to keep the skin dry. A light dusting of cornstarch can relieve itching and help keep the ink marks intact. You may rinse the treated breast in the bath or shower but don't scrub the skin or wash off any treatment-related marks. Pat the breast dry and do not apply any lotions or creams without checking with your radiation oncologist or therapist. If the skin is peeling or blistered, cortisone-containing creams or aloe vera products may be helpful.

Once the radiation treatment is finished, a moisturizing cream will reduce the itching and help to lift off any dead or peeling skin, especially around the nipple, which may remain crusty for several months.

Breast firmness

You may notice that the treated breast will be slightly more firm than the untreated one. Radiation can cause the breast to become enlarged, tender, or heavy with fluid during treatment and for about 6 to 18 months afterwards. This is particularly a problem if the breast is swollen, red, infected or heavily bruised after the surgery. The most comfortable bra is often a cotton 'sport bra' without much elastic material and without lace or seams (Figure 29). While it is important to continue wearing a bra during treatment and for several months afterwards while the breast is still tender, don't wear ones that are constricting or have underwire supports.

'Electric shocks,' burst blood vessels and scarring

It is normal to experience occasional sharp 'electric shock' sensations in the breast or chest wall. This is NOT a sign of

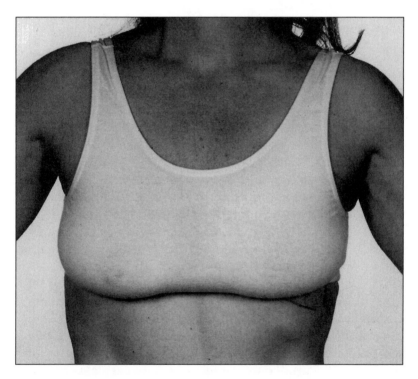

Figure 29: Wearing a supportive but nonconstricting bra is important.

Does radiation therapy itself cause cancer?

Some women are concerned that the radiation therapy itself may cause a cancer in the future. While it is true that low doses of radiation, especially in people younger than age 20, can cause cancer, the high doses used for breast cancer therapy have not been shown to increase the risk of getting cancer later on, at least not for the first 20 to 30 years after radiation therapy. One reason is probably that younger people are more susceptible to the effects of radiation, while older people (those who are much more likely to get breast cancer) are less susceptible. Rarely, unusual cancers called 'sarcomas' have been reported to develop in the treated area. This occurs in fewer than one in every 1,000 women who survive more than 10 years after initially being treated for cancer. However, since sarcomas have also been seen in women after surgery alone without radiotherapy, it is difficult to know whether the sarcomas are due to the radiation or a combination of other factors.

In summary, currently available information indicates that radiation therapy for breast cancer does not lead to a greater risk of cancers later on. Continued surveillance of treated women remains an important area of study.

---

cancer. These fleeting pains are from nerves, damaged during surgery, trying to repair themselves. Red 'burst blood vessels' may appear 18 to 24 months or more after treatment. While potentially unsightly, these are NOT a sign of cancer.

Rarely, radiation may cause severe scarring and fibrosis, with discomfort and deformity of the breast. Women who have a lot of swelling, bruising or infection of the breast after surgery are more prone to develop permanent scarring. Also, a small percentage of women (less than 1%) will develop significant scarring for no known reason.

Side effects of treating lymph nodes with radiation

The throat

If the lymph nodes near the collarbone are treated, part of the throat and the top of the lung will end up in the path of the radiation beam. You may experience a temporary sore or 'scratchy' throat or the feeling of a 'lump' in the throat. These symptoms are NOT cancer, they are just part of the treatment!

The lungs

Sometimes the lung becomes inflamed a few weeks to three months after the radiation treatment is over. This reaction is called 'radiation pneumonitis.' If you develop this condition you will experience a dry, persistent cough, fatigue and, in some cases, fever and chest pain. The pneumonitis usually clears by itself after several months, but treatment with steroids may improve symptoms if they are severe.

Scarring under the arm

Radiation may increase the amount of scarring caused by surgery in the axilla (armpit). In turn, this will increase the chance of developing arm swelling. It is important to work at regaining full use of your shoulder, and to pay careful attention to hand and arm care when the axilla is treated with both surgery and radiation therapy.

Chemotherapy

CHAPTER TWENTY-SEVEN

Chemotherapy: what is it?

'CHEMOTHERAPY' ACTUALLY MEANS the use of any drug or medication to treat disease. For example, antibiotics are a type of chemotherapy. Today, however, the word 'chemotherapy' has come to refer specifically to the drugs that are used for treating cancer. There are dozens of different chemotherapy (anticancer) drugs. Because they work in different ways, several may be given at once ('combination therapy').

The advantage of chemotherapy is it travels in the blood stream, reaching cancer cells that may be in distant organs. In contrast, surgery or radiation are local treatments that target one area only.

Chemotherapy is used in three ways in treating breast cancer: as adjuvant treatment to prevent recurrence, as the main or primary treatment for advanced (high-risk) cancers, and to relieve symptoms from cancer that has spread (metastatic cancer).

Chemotherapy as adjuvant treatment

The situation in which many patients with breast cancer receive chemotherapy is as follows: they have had surgery and the pathology report (see Chapter 13) indicates that there is a risk of the cancer recurring in other parts of the body. Chemotherapy is added to the surgery to reduce the chance of recurrence from cancer cells that cannot be detected but are presumed to still be in the body. The concept of adjuvant (preventive) therapy is discussed more completely in Chapter 23.

Chemotherapy as initial treatment for advanced (high-risk) cancer

Locally advanced cancers in the breast are considered to be high risk because they are already large when the diagnosis is made. These cancers are usually described in one of three following ways: a) the breast tumor is larger than 5.0 cm in diameter and not easily removed by surgery; b) the tumor is fixed (tethered firmly) to the chest wall muscles, the rib cage or has grown into the skin; or c) there are large, suspicious-feeling lymph nodes in the armpit. Because surgery may be unable to remove the bulk of the tumor or may require the removal of too much tissue, chemotherapy may be given first in order to shrink the tumor.

In this situation there is also a very high risk of metastatic cells outside the breast, so chemotherapy is also important to decrease the risk of recurrence elsewhere in the body.

Usually, a locally advanced cancer is treated with a combination of chemotherapy and radiation. Once the cancer has become smaller, surgery may then be done to decrease the chance of the cancer recurring in the breast. Inflammatory breast cancer (see Chapter 15) is usually treated in the same way.

Chemotherapy for treating metastatic cancer

If the breast cancer has already spread from the breast, chemotherapy may be used to slow its growth, to decrease symptoms that are caused by the cancer, and to improve the patient's quality of life. A detailed discussion of the treatment of metastatic cancer, including the use of chemotherapy, is included in Chapter 39.

How long does chemotherapy take?

Chemotherapy is usually prescribed for a three-month or six-month period. The drugs may be given intravenously (Figure 30) on one day followed by a 21-day drug-free 'rest period' and then repeated. Alternatively, a combination of oral and intravenous drugs may be given for a week or two followed by a two-week rest period. This allows for the maximum cancer-killing effect of the drugs to occur while permitting the body's blood cell counts to return to normal levels during the rest periods (see Chapter 29 on side effects of chemotherapy).

Figure 30: Getting ready for chemotherapy.

"But I've heard 'horror stories' about chemotherapy!"

Chemotherapy has a bad name due to the severe side effects women used to experience years ago when these drugs were first being developed. Because of these problems, many new drugs have since been found that control or eliminate many of these side effects. They are given at the same time as the chemotherapy drugs, thereby significantly improving the patient's well-being while the chemotherapy goes to work on the cancer cells.

Fear also stems from patients not having a clear idea WHY chemotherapy is being given. If chemotherapy is recommended as a part of your treatment, it is important for you to understand clearly the reasons for it or to ask the following questions:

- Why is the oncologist suggesting it?
- What are the goals of the chemotherapy treatment program?
- How long will the treatment take?
- What are the expected side effects?

Once you understand the reasons behind the oncologist's choice of chemotherapy, and you know what to expect, it is easier to accept some side effects knowing that the treatment is the best possible choice for your particular situation in aiming for a cure.

CHAPTER TWENTY-EIGHT

Who benefits from chemotherapy?

ADJUVANT CHEMOTHERAPY is treatment given IN ADDITION to surgery and radiation when there is a fairly high risk of the cancer recurring. The reason that chemotherapy isn't simply given to everyone is that there are side effects to the therapy, so this must be balanced against the possibility of receiving benefit from these drugs.

The risk of cancer recurrence varies with many factors, some of which we understand and some which we don't. Table 8 groups patients into broad categories of low, medium, and high risk, which makes it easier to understand the types of therapy offered to different patients.

Recommendations for adjuvant chemotherapy

In our treatment center adjuvant chemotherapy is recommended to the following groups of women:

- age less than 65 years, with axillary lymph nodes containing cancer cells AND/OR
- tumors more than 2 cm in diameter AND/OR
- cancer cells that have invaded the nerves or lymphatic or vascular channels of the breast AND/OR
- some cases in which the tumor is estrogen receptor-negative (won't respond well to hormones) and is high grade.

Table 8 **Basis for recommendations for adjuvant chemotherapy**		
Lowest risk (10% risk of recurrence after 10 years)	Moderate risk (30-60% risk of recurrence after 10 years)	Extreme risk (75-90% risk of recurrence after 10 years)
All of:	Any *one* of:	Any *one* of:
Tumor less than 1 cm	Tumor more than 2 cm	Tumor more than 5 cm with cancerous lymph nodes
plus	and/or	and/or
No cancer in nodes	Nodes contain cancer	More than 10 nodes with cancer
plus	and/or	and/or
No invasion into lymphatic vessels, blood vessels or nerves of the breast	Some invasion of lymphatic or blood vessels or nerves of the breast	Invasion into skin and chest wall and/or Inflammatory cancer
Treatment recommendations for each group*		
No adjuvant chemotherapy	Adjuvant chemotherapy	High-dose adjuvant chemotherapy
*Varies with age.		

For a number of years there were no studies that showed chemotherapy to be beneficial to postmenopausal women or women over the age of 50. Now, however, it appears that chemotherapy can decrease the number of deaths from breast cancer in some groups of women over the age of 50. These findings have changed the treatment in a number of centers. However, it must also be taken into account that older women may not tolerate chemotherapy. Considering all these factors, women between the ages of 65 and 75 years may be offered chemotherapy if their cancer has very high-risk features (see Table 8) such as a large number of lymph nodes containing cancer, a large tumor (more than 5 cm), locally advanced cancer, or high-risk cancer that will not respond well to hormone therapy.

Any recommendation for chemotherapy must be made after carefully considering the woman's general health.

Why is chemotherapy recommended for these women?

Cancer-involved lymph nodes

Cancerous lymph nodes in the armpit indicate a moderate or high risk of cancer recurrence. Surgery alone will cure only a minority of these women because the cancer cells have usually escaped outside the breast before surgery.

Unfortunately, chemotherapy is not a guarantee. Approximately three women in ten will have a long-term benefit from chemotherapy when it is included with surgery and radiotherapy. However, these numbers are very general and don't tell the whole story: women with few cancer-involved lymph nodes have fewer recurrences than women who have many nodes involved. Also, newer chemotherapy programs may be more effective than the old ones used in older studies, so today more women may be cured than in the past.

Since there is no reliable way of knowing exactly which women will be cured by chemotherapy, it is recommended for all premenopausal women with cancerous lymph nodes of the armpit and may also benefit some postmenopausal women.

What about patients whose lymph nodes are free of cancer?

Approximately seven out of ten women with no cancer in their lymph nodes will be cured by surgery and radiation. However, in the other three, breast cancer will recur even though the lymph nodes appeared to be normal in the pathology specimen.

This is when it becomes important to look at other risk factors that may help identify women at a high risk of relapse who could benefit from adjuvant chemotherapy. The pathology report contains valuable information about the cancer (see Chapter 13) and its possibility of recurrence, and should be used in making the decision of whether or not to recommend chemotherapy.

Cancer invading the lymphatics, veins and nerves of the breast

Cancer cells in the lymphatic channels, veins or nerves of the breast also increases the risk of the cancer coming back. Therefore, in some treatment centers, adjuvant chemotherapy is recommended if the pathology report describes cancer cells in these areas.

A large cancer

The size of the cancer is very important. A 1.0 cm cancer is made up of about one billion cells. The larger the cancer, the higher the risk that some of these cancer cells will have escaped from the main tumor and will be growing outside the segment removed by surgery.

When hormone therapy is less likely to work

In some cases, women with small tumors that are estrogen receptor-negative (poor responders to hormone therapy) may be considered to be at high enough risk of recurrence to consider adjuvant chemotherapy.

What's best for you

As the understanding of breast cancer improves there will be changes in the recommended treatment. As well, treatment policies may vary somewhat in different centers. Apart from these changes, what is important is for you to understand why chemotherapy has or hasn't been chosen for your particular case, and to be confident that the best possible choice of treatment has been made.

CHAPTER TWENTY-NINE

Side effects of chemotherapy

Why are there side effects?

ALL DRUGS, EVEN ANTIBIOTICS or headache tablets, have potential side effects. What counts is that the beneficial effects of a drug outweigh the problems or discomforts of its side effects. Knowing that a particular drug or combination of drugs can effectively destroy the tumor, you may be more willing to tolerate the side effects, especially since they're temporary.

It is important to be aware of possible side effects BEFORE you begin treatment and to discuss them with your doctor. This may make the chemotherapy process less mysterious and frightening, and allow you to decide for yourself whether the benefits warrant the side effects.

Although a number of side effects are predictable, others are not. For example, some chemotherapy drugs always cause hair loss while other drugs rarely affect the hair. Different people can also have different reactions to the same drug. In the last few years a number of drugs have become available which have decreased significantly the most feared side effects — nausea and vomiting.

Drug names and drug combinations

An important point to note about drug names is that all drugs have two names: a 'chemical' or 'generic' name, and a brand name. For example, headache tablets have brand names such as Aspirin® and Tylenol®, but the chemical name for Aspirin® is acetylsalicylic acid and that of Tylenol® is acetaminophen. When you are discussing a particular drug with your doctor, ask him or her to tell you both the chemical name and the brand name (write them down). Since the two names are often referred to interchangeably, being aware of both will avoid confusion.

Different chemotherapy drugs work in different ways. To take maximum advantage of this, the drugs are often given in combinations — attacking on all fronts. Because certain combinations are used frequently, you may see them referred to as abbreviations. Some typical examples are:

- AC — Adriamycin® and cyclophosphamide
- CMF — cyclophosphamide, methotrexate and 5-fluorouracil (5-FU)
- CAF (or FAC) — cyclophosphamide, Adriamycin® and 5-FU
- CEF (or FEC) — cyclophosphamide, epirubicin and 5-FU.

All of the above drug names are chemical (generic) names except for Adriamycin® (its chemical name is doxorubicin).

The side effects

Hair loss

Losing your hair is often the most difficult part of chemotherapy. At the doses used, some of the drugs such as doxorubicin (Adriamycin®) cause hair loss for everyone. Other drugs such as cyclophosphamide (Cytoxan®) may cause hair thinning for most people, but only a few lose enough to need a wig.

Hair loss occurs because the chemotherapy slows down the rapidly dividing cells of the roots of the hair. Thinning usually begins about two weeks after the first dose of chemotherapy. You will notice that you are shedding in the shower, on your brush, and on your pillow. The hair breaks at or near the skin, so the scalp may be tender. The effect may range from thinning to total baldness. The chemotherapy may also cause thinning of the hair on the rest of your body, including your eyebrows, eyelashes, arms, legs and pubic hair. The hair ALWAYS grows back, sometimes even during the chemotherapy, and it is usually already a few inches long by the third month after finishing the drugs.

Hair loss is the most upsetting event for both women and men: it is a public symbol of your cancer. Unfortunately in most situations it cannot be avoided. Fortunately it is temporary. Buy a wig before it happens and take it to your hairdresser to get it styled so you are prepared. You can also wear hats, turbans and scarves.

Although there have been attempts to decrease hair loss by scalp hypothermia (cold packs on the scalp), these are generally uncomfortable and ineffective. Furthermore, as the cold decreases blood flow to the area, many doctors are concerned that by decreasing the blood flow they also decrease the chemotherapy delivered to that area and they may be leaving a potential cancer site untreated.

Infection

White blood cells in the blood stream protect the body from infection. By about seven to ten days after each injection, many chemotherapy drugs reduce the white blood cell count. If it drops too much your body's defense mechanisms are low and you have a higher risk of getting an infection.

How can you protect yourself? You don't need to become a hermit but you should take precautions: avoid crowds and contagious diseases such as chickenpox, wash hands frequently, practice good skin care with frequent showers or baths, use a soft toothbrush, use an electric shaver rather than a razor, pay careful attention to hemorrhoids, and be on the alert for any signs of an infection. If you get a fever, sweats, a cough with yellow sputum, burning urine, a sore that will not heal, diarrhea or any signs of an infection, you should call your doctor immediately so antibiotics can be prescribed. It is rare that you would need hospitalization, but oral antibiotics may be required for about five to seven days until your white blood cells recover.

The white cell count usually recovers about 21 days after chemotherapy, which is why most courses of chemotherapy are given in sessions separated by three-week 'holidays.' If your white cell count hasn't recovered enough to make it safe to give another dose of chemotherapy according to the schedule, then treatment will be delayed or the doses will be reduced.

Anemia

The amount of red blood cells in the blood stream may also be affected by chemotherapy, but it does not usually drop too much.

Anemia may cause you to feel tired, dizzy, short of breath or chilly, so if you notice any of these symptoms you should report them to your doctor. Although you should eat well, anemia caused by chemotherapy is not usually helped by taking iron or B vitamins since the low red cell count is not caused by nutritional deficiencies but by a decreased production of red cells. If your anemia becomes severe enough to cause symptoms, your doctor may recommend a blood transfusion.

Abnormal bleeding or bruising

Platelets help to clot the blood. Chemotherapy may cause a temporary decrease of the platelet count. If this is severe enough, you may bleed easily. Again, it is rare for low platelet counts to be a significant problem, but if you notice any abnormal bleeding or bruising you should report it to your doctor. ASA (Aspirin®) or ASA-like drugs can slow down platelet function and should be taken only after checking with your doctor. However, acetaminophen (Tylenol®) does not affect the platelets and is generally all right to take in moderation.

Nausea and vomiting

Most of the chemotherapeutic drugs can cause nausea and vomiting, although some people are affected more than others. 'Antiemetic' drugs, which prevent nausea and vomiting, are usually given before the chemotherapy and every few hours afterwards for the first 24 to 48 hours. The nausea may start six to eight hours after the chemotherapy injection, or even the next day, but it is usually not a prolonged problem. Eat something before the chemotherapy and regularly thereafter because it is often better not to have an empty stomach.

The nausea may feel like morning sickness, so it is sometimes helpful to take an antiemetic, have something to eat (for instance some dry crackers) and stay in bed for an hour to prevent vomiting. Avoid odors that cause more nausea. If the drugs you are given are not effective, tell your doctor so that different or additional antiemetics can be tried.

The drugs used to prevent nausea and vomiting include ondansetron (Zofran®), prochlorperazine (Stemetil®), dimenhydrinate (Gravol®), metoclopramide (Maxeran®), and dexamethasone (Decadron®). Diphenhydramine (Benadryl®) and lorazepam (Ativan®) may also be helpful. Note that these drugs may also have side effects. For example, ondansetron (Zofran®) may cause headaches and constipation and prochlorperazine (Stemetil®) may cause restlessness that may require yet another drug, diphenhydramine (Benadryl®), for relief. The drugs may be given as pills, intravenous medications or rectal suppositories. The suppositories may be the easiest to take if you are vomiting or nauseated.

Some people also complain about stomach pain, an acidy feeling, heartburn, and a change in the taste in their mouth. These symptoms may be eased by food or antacids, but if the symptoms are severe, particularly the pain, you should notify your doctor.

Diarrhea and constipation

The anti-cancer drugs often cause some change in your bowel habits so don't be alarmed by minor disruptions. If you have severe diarrhea for more than 24 hours, or cramps, you should call your doctor because an anti-diarrheal drug may stop the problem. As well, you should be assessed to make sure this was actually related to the chemotherapy and not something totally unrelated such as a gallbladder attack or a kidney stone. If you have diarrhea, try to drink lots of clear liquids to replace the fluid that you have lost and to rest your bowels. Avoid foods such as cabbage, beans, brans and spicy foods that cause loose bowels, gas, and cramps. Milk products may also contribute to diarrhea.

Some chemotherapy drugs may cause constipation. Often this can be avoided by drinking plenty of fluids, keeping active and possibly taking a mild stool softener. If you have a severe problem, notify your doctor.

Sore mouth (mucositis)

Many of the chemotherapy drugs cause a soreness or dryness of the mouth and throat that can appear about five days after treatment begins. If this is a problem, avoid foods that irritate your mouth such as acidic, spicy or rough foods. Rinse your mouth often with baking soda and water. If your mouth gets so sore that you cannot eat, notify your doctor, as there are mouthwashes and painkillers that may ease your discomfort. People who tend to get cold sores (herpes) in addition to other mouth sores can be helped by an antiviral medication. If a white, cakey covering develops in your mouth you may have a yeast infection (Candida) which may cause mouth soreness and difficulty eating and swallowing. A special mouthwash or pill may help.

Menstrual periods and sexuality

Chemotherapy may disrupt your menstrual periods, causing them to be irregular, to stop temporarily during chemotherapy and then return, or to stop permanently. This is not predictable, but it is more likely to happen in women closer to menopause than in younger women or if you are taking six months of chemotherapy rather than three months. Menopausal symptoms of hot flashes or vaginal dryness may be troublesome; avoiding caffeine, alcohol or stress may alleviate hot flashes in some women. As well, vitamin E (800 International Units daily), clonidine (Dixarit®), evening primrose oil or other remedies may be helpful. If you are having menopausal problems, discuss them with your oncologist.

Chemotherapy drugs generally do not affect the ability or desire to have sex, although the mucosal lining of the vagina may feel dry or sore. Your libido, however, may be affected by the stress of the illness, fatigue or other symptoms, or by the changes in your body.

Prevent pregnancy during chemotherapy, but not with 'the pill'

Taking chemotherapy does not necessarily prevent pregnancy. Furthermore, IT IS IMPORTANT NOT TO GET PREGNANT WHILE ON CHEMOTHERAPY because these drugs, especially during the first three months of pregnancy, may cause damage and deformity of the fetus. While on chemotherapy, it is important to continue to use birth control measures; these should be discussed with your doctor. As your periods may be irregular, it may be difficult to predict the time of ovulation, so a combination of a barrier method (a condom or diaphragm) plus a spermicidal foam or gel is safest. Oral contraceptives are generally NOT recommended if you have breast cancer because estrogens are believed to stimulate some cancers.

General symptoms

All of the drugs may cause skin changes such as dryness, spots, increased sun sensitivity, or rashes. If you're going out in the sun wear protective clothing, including a sun hat. Many women complain about dry, gritty eyes which can be eased by eye drops or artificial tears. Other women complain of a flu-like feeling or of feeling cold for one to three days after the chemotherapy starts.

If the drug contains a dye (for example Adriamycin®, which is red) your urine may change color the day after you start chemotherapy as you excrete the drug. You do not need to take special precautions in the bathroom, as the chemotherapy drugs are not dangerous to anyone else: it is not like being radioactive! You should drink plenty of fluids to ensure a good urine flow and to prevent bladder irritation.

Some women develop joint or muscle aches and pains. These often begin after the chemotherapy is finished and can last several months. Fortunately, they are usually temporary and can be relieved with exercise or anti-inflammatory medications.

Certain drugs may cause tingling in the fingers and toes, and some people report a loss of muscle strength and a change in their sense of balance. This also should be temporary: if it is not, or if it interferes with your activities, report it to your doctor.

Other rare side effects may also occur, so if you experience a new problem that is unexpected you should report it to your doctor, as it may or may not be related to the chemotherapy. If you have finished your treatments and are on follow-up, you should probably report it to your family doctor, since your complaints may be unrelated to the therapy.

Other considerations while taking chemotherapy

While you are on chemotherapy you can eat whatever you like. However, if you are taking some other medication for another condition, your doctor should verify that it may be continued. Although some physicians and nutritionists recommend total abstinence from alcohol, an occasional glass of wine or beer is usually OK, but check with your doctor.

Fatigue levels vary. Some women are able to continue their normal activities and continue working throughout the chemotherapy. Others find the chemotherapy so physically or emotionally draining they need to take a leave from work. Although it is recommended that you remain as active as you can while on chemotherapy, you will need some extra rest. Since it's hard to predict how much rest you will need, it may be worthwhile to sit down with your family or your employer and warn them that there may be low-energy days.

Hormone Therapy

CHAPTER THIRTY

Hormone therapy: What is it and who benefits from it?

Hormones and hormone therapy

What are female hormones?

THE FEMALE HORMONES, estrogen and progesterone, control many of the female- and sex-related processes of the body, such as growth of female genitals and breasts, development of the female body shape and regulation of the menstrual cycle.

What is the relationship between hormones and breast cancer?

Estrogen not only stimulates the growth of the breasts, but it also appears to encourage the growth of some, but not all, breast tumors.

What is hormone therapy?

Hormone therapy for breast cancer is a form of whole-body (systemic) treatment that is used as adjuvant therapy or as treatment for cancer recurrence. The term 'hormone therapy' refers to a number of different treatments designed to reduce the level of female hormones in the body. These include the use of drugs, surgical removal of the ovaries (the ovaries produce estrogen in premenopausal women), or destruction of the ovaries by radiation (ablation of the ovaries). Hormone treatment is systemic because it affects hormone levels in the entire body. Changing the hormone levels affects the cancer cells and slows their growth. Hormone therapy may also be referred to as 'anti-estrogen therapy.' The most widely used and tested anti-estrogen drug is tamoxifen (Novaldex®, Tamofen®, etc.). Since this is the initial form of hormone therapy that most women take, this chapter will discuss the recommendations for this drug in detail.

Who should receive adjuvant tamoxifen?

As always, before deciding on any type of adjuvant therapy, the woman with breast cancer must be assessed to estimate her chances of the cancer recurring. The stage of the cancer must be reviewed (Chapter 17), taking into account the size of the cancer, the presence of cancer-involved lymph nodes, and the finding of lymphatic, vascular or neural cancerous invasion in the breast. Table 9 shows the assessment of cancer broadly categorized as low, moderate and high risk of recurrence, with the recommendations for or against adjuvant tamoxifen therapy in each category.

It is important to realize that these risk categories are useful, but are just general guidelines. Each woman's case is different and her risk of recurrence must be assessed based on other details in the pathology report in addition to these features. Therefore, a woman's risk may fit one of these categories exactly or be somewhere in between.

Tamoxifen works best in older women

With tamoxifen, the age of the woman is important: studies show that hormone therapy is more beneficial to post-menopausal women than premenopausal women.

'ER-positive' or 'ER-negative'? Which type of tumor does tamoxifen attack best?

The pathologist can test a piece of the tumor using a chemical test to estimate how well the cancer is likely to respond to the anti-estrogen drug. This is done by measuring the amount of 'estrogen receptors' (ER) on the cancer cell. (The estrogen receptors are where the estrogen attaches to the tumor. The anti-estrogen drug interferes with the receptor, preventing the estrogen from 'landing' on the tumor.)

Table 9 Recommendations for the use of adjuvant tamoxifen		
Low risk of recurrence	Moderate risk of recurrence	High risk of recurrence
All of:	Any *one* of:	Any *one* of:
Tumor less than 1 cm	Tumor more than 2 cm	Tumor more than 5 cm with cancerous lymph nodes
plus	and/or	and/or
No cancer in lymph nodes	1 to 7 lymph nodes with cancer	More than 8 lymph nodes with cancer
plus	and/or	and/or
No invasion into lymph channels, blood vessels of the breast, or into lymph nodes	Some invasion into lymph channels, blood vessels of the breast, or into lymph nodes	Skin invasion Chest wall invasion Inflammatory cancer
Recommendations for postmenopausal women		
No adjuvant tamoxifen	Adjuvant tamoxifen If ER-positive: tamoxifen with or without chemotherapy If ER-negative: chemotherapy plus tamoxifen	High-dose chemotherapy plus tamoxifen
Recommendations for premenopausal women		
No adjuvant therapy	Chemotherapy If ER-positive: not yet known. Tamoxifen studies in progress If ER-negative: no tamoxifen	High-dose chemotherapy plus tamoxifen
ER = estrogen receptor; see text		

In general, the higher the estrogen receptor level, the more responsive the tumor will be to tamoxifen. If the pathologist measures very few estrogen receptors (less than 10 to 15 units), then this means that the tumor is not being affected very much by the estrogen in the body to begin with, so anti-estrogen therapy may not have as much benefit in these patients.

Since the piece of tumor to be tested for estrogen receptor level must be at least 0.5 cm, very small cancers cannot be tested by this method.

Another type of test for estrogen receptor content of a cancer is called 'immunoperoxidase staining.' With this test, the ER content of the tumor is reported as 0, +1, +2, or +3, with 0 representing virtually no estrogen receptor content and +3 a high ER content.

Other questions about tamoxifen

What is the dose?

Tamoxifen is usually taken daily as a single 20 mg dose or as a 10 mg dose twice a day. Today, most centers recommend continuing tamoxifen treatment for five years.

Why don't postmenopausal women at low risk of cancer recurrence take tamoxifen?

Tamoxifen, like other therapy, does have some side effects that need to be considered and, at present, this group has not yet been proven to benefit sufficiently from the drug to warrant the small but real risk of side effects. This may change, however, as new studies of tamoxifen are completed.

Does tamoxifen have other beneficial effects?

At menopause, women's chances of getting heart disease begin to increase. Tamoxifen seems to protect postmenopausal women from this increased risk of heart attacks by maintaining cholesterol and lipids at levels similar to those of premenopausal women. It also slows the loss of calcium from the bones and may reduce the chance of osteoporosis. However, protection from heart disease or osteoporosis is not a sufficient reason to recommend adjuvant tamoxifen therapy.

Side effects of
hormone therapy

Do hormone therapies have side effects?

As with all other drug treatments, there are potential side effects associated with hormone treatments. These must be carefully discussed and considered before starting treatment. The side effects may depend on the dose or length of treatment.

Tamoxifen

Tamoxifen is an estrogen as well as an anti-estrogen. This means that it acts like an estrogen on some normal tissues, but blocks the estrogen receptors of the cancer cells.

Many women have no side effects from tamoxifen. Others notice some side effects, several of which are listed below.

Hot flashes are more pronounced in premenopausal women and are often temporary.

Vaginal discharge: this may be clear or whitish. If you have a bloody discharge it is abnormal and should be investigated by your physician.

Weight gain is common and usually only a few pounds.

Facial hair: this is not common and is usually very sparse.

Phlebitis: this is an inflamed vein that contains a blood clot. It occurs in about 1% of women taking tamoxifen for five years. It is dangerous because the clot can dislodge and travel to other parts of the body, especially the lungs, causing a pulmonary embolus (blockage of a blood vessel at the lungs). Phlebitis and blood clots are more frequent in women who are also getting chemotherapy at the same time as the tamoxifen, in women with a previous history of phlebitis, and in women who have other risk factors such as a history of smoking. If you have a swollen or painful leg or calf muscle, see your doctor. If the diagnosis confirms a blood clot, medication may be prescribed to dissolve the clot and tamoxifen should probably be stopped.

Continuation of menstruation: for premenopausal women, ovulation and menses may continue so birth control precautions should be maintained. The drug's effect on a fetus is not known.

Nausea or vomiting, loss of appetite: these are rare and usually temporary.

Rash, skin dryness and hair loss: these are very rare.

Headache, depression and dizziness: also rare.

Fatigue and malaise: rare.

Hypercalcemia (high calcium levels in the blood): this usually occurs only if there are bone metastases. If you get very thirsty, constipated, nauseated and confused, your blood calcium level should be checked.

Flare-up of pain: metastatic cancer may react to the tamoxifen by becoming more painful. This is called a 'flare reaction' and is usually temporary. It is considered to be a good sign, indicating that the cancer is responding to the tamoxifen.

Endometrial (uterine) cancer: some women taking tamoxifen have been found to develop cancer of the endometrium. At the currently recommended dose of 20 mg per day for five years, approximately two women per 1,000 will develop endometrial cancer each year. This is two to three times higher than the risk in the general population of women not taking tamoxifen. For women with invasive breast cancers larger than 1 cm, the chance of developing endometrial cancer while taking tamoxifen is less than the benefit of avoiding a recurrence of breast cancer by taking tamoxifen. However, if you have any unexplained vaginal bleeding you should see your doctor. As well, you should have an annual pelvic examination.

Liver tumors: these have occurred in women taking tamoxifen but are very rare and may be benign.

Other anti-estrogens

New anti-estrogens are being developed that act in a similar way as tamoxifen but may have different side effects. For example, droloxifene, toremifene and trioxifene have been shown to have some effect on breast cancer and are being tested to assess their side effects and potential usefulness. Other anti-estrogens are also being tested to see if they have advantages over tamoxifen, both in terms of decreased side effects and increased effectiveness.

Progestins (e.g. megestrol acetate [Megace®])

Although megestrol acetate is commonly used, it is not entirely clear how it works. However, this and other progestins have been shown to be effective in treating metastatic breast cancer, with an overall response rate of about 28%. Megestrol and high-dose medroxyprogesterone acetate have been shown to be as effective as tamoxifen.

Megace® is well tolerated. The following side effects may occur.

Weight gain, the major side effect, occurs in 20% to 50% of patients. The weight gain may be only a few pounds or may be more, and is related to the dose of the drug. The higher the dose the more frequent and greater the weight gain. Both an increase in appetite and fluid retention are responsible for the extra pounds.

Vaginal bleeding occurs in 5% to 10% of women. It sometimes happens while taking the drug but occurs more often when it is discontinued. A vaginal discharge may also occur.

Hot flashes are much less common than with tamoxifen, but may occur.

High blood pressure is rare.

High blood sugar level: patients with diabetes who already have elevated blood sugars may need to adjust their diabetes medication if the sugars get too high due to the megestrol.

Nausea and vomiting have been reported in about 10% of women on megestrol.

Headaches and depression may occur infrequently.

Rash and itch have been reported.

Increased level of calcium is rare but can occur in women with bone metastases.

Rarely, a mild decrease in the white blood cell count and/or platelet counts have been reported.

Fluid retention, which is usually mild.

Other progestins such as medroxyprogesterone acetate may cause an increase in acne or facial hair, constipation, muscle cramps, skin abscesses, increased sweating, mild fatigue, and congestive heart failure as well as the same side effects as megestrol. Hair loss has also been reported.

Anti-progestins

This new class of drug has shown some effectiveness but requires further testing. An example is mifepristone (RU 486) which is known as the medication developed in France to induce abortions.

Aminoglutethimide (Cytadren®)

Aminoglutethimide has been used for the treatment of breast cancer since the 1970s and is an effective agent, particularly for metastases in bone, skin or lymph nodes.

Because high doses of aminoglutethimide can block the production of one of the body's hormones, cortisone, you may need to take daily doses of cortisone in a pill form with the aminoglutethimide. This will depend on the dose of aminoglutethimide prescribed.

Side effects of this drug are listed below.

Fatigue: this may improve the longer the drug is taken.

Dizziness: this may occur more often if you leap out of bed or stand up quickly. This too, often gets better with time.

Rash, which may or may not be itchy, often occurs when the drug is started but goes away after a few days. Your doctor may decrease the dose, stop the drug for a week, or just have you continue taking it depending on how irritating your rash is.

Nausea and vomiting occur in about 15% of women but usually is mild and temporary.

Neurological complaints: rarely, aminoglutethimide can cause a wobbly gait which is often temporary but should be reported to your doctor.

Fever, sweating, and leg cramps are rare.

Decreased levels of white blood cells or platelets are rare.

Facial swelling or low or high blood pressure are very rare.

New drugs of the same class as aminoglutethimide (known as an 'aromatase inhibitor') are being developed to try to find others with fewer side effects. A number of these are already being tested and may prove to be effective.

Androgens

Androgens are male hormones that can be used to treat metastatic breast cancer. Fluoxymesterone (Halotesin®) has been commonly used and is effective. There are a number of side effects.

A masculinizing effect may include scalp hair loss, growth of facial hair, lowering of the voice, increase in size of the clitoris and increase in body hair. The extent of the side effects depends on the dose, the duration of treatment and the individual. These effects may not completely reverse when the drug is stopped.

Weight gain is usually mild.

Nausea and decreased appetite may occur occasionally, and even less so with low doses of the drug.

What can be done about side effects?

Listing all of the side effects of these drugs is depressing. The thing to remember is that most women do not experience many of these side effects. The positive side, of course, is that the drugs are being given because of their beneficial anti-cancer effects. Each woman should evaluate the risks and benefits of treatment on an individual basis with her doctors.

If you experience any side effects it is important to discuss them with your doctors and nurses, since they may be able to offer helpful suggestions or remedies. The three commonest side effects of hormone therapy are mild nausea, hot flashes and vaginal dryness/irritation. The nausea often goes away after two to three weeks. Some practical tips regarding control of mild nausea and decreased appetite are described in Chapter 35; more severe nausea and vomiting are usually treated with drugs.

Hot flashes can sometimes be reduced in severity or frequency by avoiding caffeine, alcohol and stress or by altering the time of day that you take your medication. Some drugs can be taken in a divided dose which may reduce hot flashes (for example, take tamoxifen in doses of 10 mg twice a day instead of 20 mg at night). Low-dose clonidine (Dixarit®), a prescription medication, may help reduce the hot flashes. Many women have developed 'home remedies' which seem to work for them and, although not proven, vitamin E (800 I.U. daily) and evening primrose oil, among others, have been helpful.

Vaginal dryness and irritation can make intercourse uncomfortable or impossible. A water-soluble lubricating jelly (for example, K-Y® or Muko®; available in your drugstore) may be helpful. This jelly should be applied to the vaginal opening and to the head of the penis to make initiation of intercourse easier. Petroleum-based jellies (i.e. Vaseline) are not advised since they are messy and get sticky with rubbing, making matters worse. If symptoms are very severe and the above is unsuccessful, occasionally it is helpful to use a small amount of estrogen vaginal cream applied to the opening of the vagina daily for two weeks (not injected into the vagina as usually recommended) and then about once per week. Some of the estrogen may be absorbed into the blood stream, but one has to balance quality of life against any small potential risk due to the estrogen.

Inhibitors of the pituitary hormones

The pituitary gland makes a number of hormones that control specific glands such as the ovary. Several drugs have been used to try to decrease the levels of these 'controlling' hormones. The most promising are medications that interfere with FSH (follicular stimulating hormone) and LH (luteinizing hormone), hormones that control the ovaries. Without FSH and LH the ovary stops making many of the estrogens. Studies are being done with drugs that consist of a combination of tamoxifen and these inhibitors of pituitary hormones, for example, leuprolide (Lupron®) and goserelin (Zoladex®).

These drugs have very few side effects. Menstrual periods will stop in premenopausal women but this may take three to four months. Hot flashes and other menopausal symptoms may occur but will stop when the drug is discontinued. Rare instances of nausea, depression, increased bone pain, and swelling of the eyelids or breasts have also been reported.

PART THREE | **Beyond the initial phase of treatment**

Coping with Cancer

CHAPTER THIRTY-TWO

Living with a diagnosis of breast cancer

by Carolyn Baker, RN

ALTHOUGH EVERY PERSON with cancer and every family member is unique, the road each must travel is well worn by the millions of others who have come before. It is a journey marked by hope and despair, courage and fear, humor and anger, and constant uncertainty. While the body undergoes tests and treatments, the mind searches for its own way of coping. This section is dedicated to the emotional effects of the diagnosis and treatment of cancer — the side of cancer that neither surgery nor chemotherapy nor radiation can treat.

Is there a 'right way' to feel after receiving a cancer diagnosis?

Many women are concerned that the thoughts and feelings that they experience following a diagnosis of cancer are somehow abnormal or crazy and that there must be a 'right way' to feel. This couldn't be further from the truth. There is no one way to feel. Reactions to the diagnosis can span the full range of human emotion: anger, anxiety, uncertainty, hopelessness, helplessness, depression, a feeling of isolation, vulnerability, relief that there really is something wrong, and even guilt that one has somehow contributed to the development of her own disease, or delayed in bringing it to a doctor's attention.

It is important to realize that the initial reaction to the diagnosis will be followed by other feelings. It is an emotional process or journey that occurs. Just as we go through a series of 'stages' in accepting the loss of a loved one, we pass through a number of emotional levels on our way to acknowledging the diagnosis of cancer. First, there is often disbelief in the diagnosis, denial that it is true, and anger at being 'singled out.' Finally, there is usually an acknowledgement that 'Yes, I do have cancer.' Why we go through these stages is difficult to know. Psychologists postulate that the time required to progress from disbelief to acknowledgement may offer protection by creating time and space for adjustment.

> 'I felt shocked...numb...like it wasn't real. I don't think I really felt anything for a week and then I felt betrayed.'
> 'I decided that the doctors had made a mistake and that any minute someone would come out and say it had all been an unfortunate mistake.'

Denial is often a prominent response early in the cancer experience. It is a defense against fear and helps to maintain emotional equilibrium. The individual believes that the diagnosis is wrong, that it doesn't have anything to do with her. It is not uncommon to hear people comment, 'I think she's in denial,' as if there may be something unusual and potentially dangerous about this reaction. In fact, some degree of denial is normal and is probably necessary to protect oneself and to maintain the hope needed to participate in daily life. However, it is important to recognize that denial is healthy only as long as it does not interfere with seeking medical care or participating in appropriate treatment.

> 'At some level I had to distance myself from the reality of the cancer in order to listen to the information that I was being given. I had to think that this was about someone else...It really protected me but it drove my husband crazy.'

Expressions of very strong emotion are to be expected and they may range from anger and bitterness to frank hostility which may be directed at anyone and anything.

> 'I was angry at everyone...God in particular... I hadn't done anything to deserve this.'
> 'I was furious. I really didn't think that I needed to get cancer in order to be better at my job or to be a better person. Someone was playing a cruel joke.'

Fortunately, most people will emerge from the storm of emotions to reach a point of equilibrium and acknowledgement, although it is common to move back and forth from one 'stage' to another. Many think about having cancer in the past tense. This helps the woman to keep the cancer from dominating her life and allows her to remain more positive, even if she is well aware of the possibility of recurrence.

> 'Have I accepted my diagnosis of cancer? I don't know. After six months I still often wish it wasn't so, think that it isn't so and remember that it is. It's a constant back-and-forth.'

Coping with cancer

Every person has a unique tool box of coping strategies that we add to over a lifetime. Most will find what they need to meet the challenge of cancer.

> 'How did I cope initially? I don't know, really... I guess I did the things that I've done in other tough situations...I turned to my family and friends, then the nurses and doctors.'

There are as many coping skills as there are people. Seeking information, turning to family, friends and others in a similar situation for support, developing a partnership with the health care team, maintaining hope, and learning stress management techniques are all means by which the coping 'mindset' develops.

Seeking information

Appropriate information can help to allay much of the anxiety and fear associated with the unknown. The type and amount required varies with the wants and needs of the woman and her family. Generally, people want to know about diagnostic tests, treatment plan (purpose, expected results, side effects, length of time and scheduling), and prognosis. Essential but often neglected information concerns how the disease and treatment are likely to affect the person's daily life. Your local chapter of the Cancer Society is an excellent place to look for this kind of help. Most local chapters of the Society provide booklets, seminars, stress management training, and self-help groups for individuals with cancer and their families.

Of course, the health care team is a critical provider of information pertinent to your particular problem. When attending appointments with members of the health care team, don't be afraid to ask questions. They will be expecting it. Prepare a list; otherwise, you may forget important points that you have been wondering about. Write down the answers and, if you wish, take someone along to help you remember what was said. The early phase of diagnosis and treatment can be somewhat of a daze and having a spare pair of ears around is very helpful.

Telling others

In most cases, your family and close friends will learn sooner or later that you have cancer. It is usually best to disclose the information yourself, according to your own schedule. Confiding fears and hopes is an important part of developing the coping mindset, and in the long run it is easier than trying to conceal these important feelings.

There are some situations in which it may be best not to tell. Family members who are too old, too young, or too emotionally fragile may have difficulty accepting or understanding the situation. However, it is quite extraordinary how most people can summon the courage to adapt to the reality of a potentially life-threatening illness, even when it involves someone whom they love very much.

Sometimes family members are the first to learn the diagnosis and they will occasionally attempt to shield the person with cancer from the information in what is usually a misguided but well meant attempt to protect her from the pain of knowing.

In certain instances, such as when the woman is extremely old or very ill and cannot understand, this is sensible. In the vast majority of cases, however, it is better, and her right, for her to know. Otherwise, important relationships that should be strengthened become strained and artificial as loving family members and friends try to skirt the issue and discuss only superficial matters. Worse than that, in almost all such cases, the woman finds out anyway, all too often at an inopportune and harmful moment. Don't let this happen. Given the truth about the situation, sensitively presented, the woman with cancer is permitted the opportunity to evolve naturally toward the point of acknowledgement and can set her mind on important priorities. Everyone is owed that much.

Women usually have a lot of anxiety about how best to explain to their children about the cancer when they are trying to cope, themselves, with what it all means. They are worried about being able to care for their children during treatment, and whether they will be around to help them grow up. The goal in telling children is to give them opportunities to ask questions about the disease and to express their feelings about it. While we all wish to shield our children from 'bad news,' it is better that they experience pain in a way that they understand and can talk about with their parents than to cope with sorrow on their own in forms that become embellished by their imagination. Moreover, if they are denied knowledge of the cause of why there has been great disruption in the family, they may become confused and hurt and mistakenly believe that they are responsible. There are several excellent books available which can help you to explain 'cancer' to children of various ages (see Additional Reading).

Support groups

In most cities and towns there are support groups consisting of people with cancer and trained professionals who manage the sessions. The professionals provide a forum where the person with cancer can be open about her thoughts and feelings, and can discover that these are normal and acceptable. Other members of the group often suggest alternative ways to deal with difficult issues, ways that have helped them. Seeing others who are coping with similar situations can aid in identifying solutions to problems which seem overwhelming initially. In addition, membership in a formal group may give the person with cancer the means to overcome a feeling of helplessness by offering assistance to others.

> 'Although my family was supportive, I felt as if they couldn't possibly understand what it was like for me. I needed to talk to someone else who had cancer. That doesn't mean that you shouldn't talk to your family but it's different when you talk to another survivor. In the Living with Cancer Group, I found that I could give something back...which was very important as it was the first time in a long time that I felt useful.'

Reach to Recovery

In addition to formal support groups, most women will benefit from meeting with a 'survivor.' The Reach to Recovery program of the Cancer Society is an invaluable resource to the woman with a new diagnosis of breast cancer. Ideally, this contact with a Reach to Recovery volunteer should occur while the woman is considering surgery or still in hospital.

Reach to Recovery volunteers have 'been there.' They provide women with a wealth of information about living with breast cancer — from talking to family and friends, to buying a bathing suit with suitable support. They also provide a 'shoulder to cry on.'

You do not need to wait for a referral from a doctor or nurse to initiate a Reach to Recovery visit. Any woman (or her family and friends) can call the Cancer Society to request a Reach to Recovery visit either before surgery, during the hospital stay, or afterwards.

> 'When the volunteer walked through the door and said that she was ten years out from diagnosis, I felt an enormous weight melt away. She gave me more hope with her presence than anyone else had with their words.'

Developing a partnership with the health care team

At one time, patients and families were considered to be silent members of the health care team, if indeed they were considered team members at all. Today, people with cancer are encouraged to take an active role in treatment planning.

The first step in developing a partnership with the health care team is to know who the players are and what each one has to offer. This can be a challenging task as, over time, there are often many different specialists involved in the care of the patient and family. It is important to identify one team member who will serve as the leader: often the family doctor, the oncologist (cancer specialist) or a specialist nurse. It doesn't matter who assumes the role as long as he or she is able to relate to the woman and her family and will be there for the duration. This person should be available at regular intervals, or when required, to listen to concerns, to direct questions to the appropriate professionals, and to serve as a guide and support.

The second important step is to participate in decision-making about treatment. Although this may seem impossible because of what appears to be an overwhelming amount of information that needs to be taken into account, a skilled professional should be able to simplify the facts so that two or three alternatives can be presented at any stage of treatment.

> 'I had a life-threatening illness and I was being asked whether I wanted this treatment or that treatment. I felt that my life was on the line if I made the wrong decision. I didn't know whether or not I wanted that responsibility. Then I realized that I knew me better than anyone else and that knowledge would be helpful in making a good decision.'

No matter how complex your problem may seem, your team members are expected to be able to help you through the decision-making processes by providing you with the framework of the 'big picture,' thereby simplifying decisions. His or her ability to explain things is essential in providing you with the information you need to participate. Once a few of the initial choices are made based on such information, you will have some time to seek additional resources and pursue the educational process that will support you later on.

Participating in decision-making means listening to the options, identifying their advantages and disadvantages, and comparing them to your own values and aspirations and those of your family. Some women will want to discuss all of the options, perhaps seeking a second opinion before making an informed decision with or without their families. Others might be uncomfortable making the final decision, but can still participate by clarifying their values and wishes so that the final recommendations for treatment can be tailored to their needs.

The third step in developing a partnership with the health care team is to participate in the treatment plan — managing the side effects of the treatment, reporting changes in condition, attending follow-up appointments, providing team members with feedback about how things are progressing, and using the services and supports that are available.

A note about changing doctors

Clearly, excellent communication between each woman and her doctor is critically important to the successful adaptation to the diagnosis and treatment. Unfortunately, some physicians never learn to speak comfortably with their patients or families and in the name of some sort of professionalism let people down by not 'being there' for them when tough choices have to be made. Although such physicians may appear to be abrupt, aloof and uncaring, this is not usually the case. Nevertheless, if this problem creates a barrier, ask your family doctor to refer you to someone else. Remember, you almost always have a choice in who treats you, so don't be afraid to find someone who you are comfortable with. Keep in mind, however, that a decision to change physicians should be based on reality and not on a quest to find a doctor who will promise a cure and guarantee to relieve all your fears.

When friends don't call

Lost and strained friendships can be a particularly painful aspect of dealing with cancer. Friends may not call for a variety of reasons. For most, it is because they feel that they will have so little to say that will help, and they fear that instead they might say something hurtful. Others may be afraid that they will not be able to respond appropriately to your change of appearance, or they are fearful of facing the possibility of your death and the eventuality of their own.

> 'I see that my friends don't know how to talk to me, and they shy away from me.'

None of these reasons have anything to do with your friends' view of your worth and, indeed, some may be suffering themselves from the loss of their normal relationship with you. If you believe it is discomfort that is keeping a particular friend from visiting, you might try a phone call to dissolve the barrier. This often reassures them that you are still the same person that they liked before, and that you understand their difficulty. However, don't expect to change or enlighten everyone. We all have our own emotional capabilities and timetables and some people will not be comforted sufficiently for them to maintain the relationship as it was before. You will find that different friends will provide suppport in different ways at different times. Also, you will make new friends along the way who are participating in the same treatment process.

Sexuality

Sexuality need not be affected by the diagnosis of breast cancer but it often is. Many women feel mutilated by the surgery and uncomfortable with their bodies. Also, treatment can cause fatigue and other symptoms that decrease desire. In addition, the onset of treatment-induced menopause may make intercourse uncomfortable due to vaginal dryness.

The whole process of the diagnosis and treatment may make a woman less interested in sex. Her focus may be on other issues or she may feel depressed. This is normal and needs to be openly discussed with her partner. Her partner may also be frightened about losing and/or hurting her. A common myth is that cancer may be contagious. This is entirely false.

By recognizing these changes and seeking counselling if necessary, these feelings may improve with time and understanding. A satisfying sexual relationship is possible after breast cancer.

Maintaining hope

Hope is a crucial tool for people with cancer and their families. It is the internal resource that permits one to cope with the stresses associated with diagnosis and treatment. Loss of hope reduces one's ability to adjust to the situation.

Hope means different things to different people, and tends to change over time depending on the stage of the disease and treatment:

> 'There is always hope, it just changes. First you hope that you don't have cancer, then you hope that the cancer is curable or at least treatable. Then you hope for time and finally, you hope for a good going. If you lose hope you give up.'

Maintaining and nurturing hope is a strategy that can allay anxiety, depression and fear. Nurturing hope means focusing on the present and what is immediately ahead, rather than on the future or the past, neither of which can be changed. While this reorientation of focus can be difficult in our future-oriented society, it can help manage the daily challenges of cancer treatment.

Hope can be affected by the behavior of others. Those around the woman and her family must not only be aware of the hopes that are held but should also attempt to share them or to shape them into more attainable goals. Family members and friends can support the idea that being hopeful is a good thing, and they should not classify hope as being false.

> 'Be prepared for the worst but hope for the best. There is no such thing as false hope. Every day I hope for a miracle, but that doesn't stop me from continuing my treatment nor would it stop me from acceptance if my treatment is no longer working. If you took my hope away I don't know if I would want to continue...'

Hope is not based on false optimism or benign reassurance, but is built on the belief that better days or moments can come in spite of the situation.

CHAPTER THIRTY-THREE

Physiotherapy:
An important part of recovery
by Cynthia Webster, BSR

Why is physiotherapy important?

THE GOAL OF PHYSIOTHERAPY is to help each woman regain her maximum physical function and return to as normal a life as possible.

It is important to realize that the problems encountered during the treatment of breast cancer are not the same as sports injuries or problems due to aging. Specific treatments and exercises have been developed to deal with the specific problems related to breast cancer. Physical therapists are available to help and guide your physical recovery. You can do it!

What does physiotherapy involve?

Most physiotherapy involves doing exercises to improve muscle or joint mobility, and using simple treatments to reduce arm swelling and pain.

Will any physical therapist do?

No. Not all physical therapists have specific knowledge of breast cancer and the disabilities caused by its treatment. For example, surgery and radiation therapy can injure the muscles and nerves of the chest wall and shoulder joint, and chemotherapy can cause joint and muscle pain. Therefore, the physical therapist must understand how medical and surgical procedures affect the body and be able to advise you on the best program for recovery. When selecting your physiotherapist it is prudent to ask her, 'How many women with breast cancer do you treat?' To stay current, she should have a record of treating breast cancer cases every week.

Typical daily activities: what's OK, what's not after surgery involving removal of lymph nodes

'YES' activities

- **Carrying things:** Shoulder bags and heavy hand bags should be carried on the opposite shoulder. Whenever possible, fanny packs or waist pouches should be worn to take the uneven weight off the shoulders. Briefcases should be carried in the opposite hand, without a lot of weight in them. Avoid carrying large suitcases; use ones with wheels. Also, it's better to push, not pull, any heavy item, including a golf cart, with your arm on your surgical side.

- **Ironing:** This is a difficult, resisted exercise. Most of the movement is produced by the pectoral muscles and shoulder stabilizers. To begin ironing again, put a timer on for 15 minutes. When the timer goes off, stop and change activities.

- **Dishes:** Regular cleaning is not a problem. Heavy scrubbing of pots and pans requires care during the first six weeks after surgery.

  If you are undergoing chemotherapy and radiation, limit the amount of work that puts a strain on your arms and upper body.

'NO' activities

- **Push-ups:** The strain on the shoulder is too much for the first three to six months.

- **Push-up positions during sexual intercourse:** Leaning down and forward, supporting your weight on your arms is hard on the shoulder and chest muscles, and may cause pain and swelling of the arm.

How soon should physiotherapy begin?

Planning your physiotherapy can begin even before surgery. Since the goal is to prevent disability and help you to return to your normal activities as soon as possible, a consultation before surgery will allow you to begin your exercises as early as possible. Active exercise programs can start within the first weeks following surgery and should continue while you are undergoing any type of adjuvant therapy.

Regaining full arm and shoulder movement after surgery

Whether you have a lumpectomy or total mastectomy, if some of the lymph nodes in the armpit are removed then the muscles and other tissues of the chest wall, shoulder and arm will be affected. Some women may develop a loss of shoulder mobility. To determine what your full shoulder movement should be, compare your nonaffected side with your affected side. Unless you have full shoulder movement right after surgery you may benefit from physiotherapy.

Other women develop 'tethering,' which is an attachment of the tissue under the skin to other tissues beneath, which feels like having tight cords under the arm extending even as far as the wrist. Tethering restricts the ability to lift the arm or straighten the elbow. The physiotherapist will teach you specific movements, usually slow stretches, designed to release the tethering and retrain the muscles. In some instances laser therapy is also used to release the tethering.

You also need to learn how much exercise and activity is beneficial. Too much exercise can trigger a muscle spasm or excessive pain.

Retraining should begin with simple stretching exercises, gradually including exercises that resist movement, for example, with weights. The exercises should be continued until the shoulder can move normally and the muscles have recovered their full strength. The best way to maintain this full range of movement is to incorporate a regular exercise program into your daily life. Care must be taken not to overwork the arm and shoulder if the armpit lymph nodes were removed, since straining or over-stretching can cause pain and arm swelling.

Your program should include not only exercises for the shoulder but also for the neck, back and chest.

Regaining muscle strength and easing muscle spasms

Muscles can lose strength and tone whenever they are directly affected by surgery or radiation, or by periods of immobilization. A muscle that is both weak and tight will go into spasm easily and cause a lot of pain. Even muscles that are not directly in the treated area may be affected. 'Postural fatigue syndrome,' triggered by weakness, can cause the muscles of the shoulder, neck, trunk and even pelvis to become fatigued and then go into spasm, causing pain and sometimes interrupting sleep. Often, the pain from the spasm triggers a deep fear that the cancer is back. It isn't, and you can learn to control the pain. The physical therapist will help you to understand how muscles function, why spasms occur, how to prevent and control muscle spasm, and how to break the spasm cycle.

Isometric exercises are one of the safest and easiest methods of controlling muscle spasms. These involve repeatedly contracting and then relaxing the muscles. These exercises do not interfere with the healing of surgical stitches (sutures). Although it may be difficult to start moving the painful part, careful consistent, daily exercise aimed at defined goals can produce dramatic results. Several exercises are outlined later in this chapter.

Controlling arm swelling

Normally, tissue fluid drains from the arm, through the lymph nodes in the armpit and back into the circulation (Chapter 1). This normal flow is slowed down or blocked if some of the lymph nodes are removed by surgery, or scar tissue has formed from radiotherapy, infection or the cancer itself. The tissue fluid then accumulates and the arm swells (lymphedema or edema). An important goal of physiotherapy is prevention and treatment of arm swelling. Unfortunately, many women with breast cancer endure persistent arm swelling because of the mistaken belief that little can be done to reduce it or because they initially receive inadequate treatment for it.

Edema appears most often within the first year after surgery but can develop at any time. It can limit the arm's mobility and, in severe cases, impair finger and nerve function.

Early signs of edema are aching of the shoulder, or a feeling like a tight band around the upper arm. Early treatment is essential to control the edema and restore the arm to its normal size and function.

The most important aspect of lymphedema is prevention. Because the lymph nodes are where the body fights infection, once lymph nodes in the armpit are removed it is important to try to reduce infection or injury of the hand or arm to help prevent aggravating the lymphedema. Special attention should be given to avoiding punctures, cuts, burns and insect bites for the rest of your life. If they do occur, the wound must be cleaned and protected. Also, one should wear long-sleeved clothing and gloves when working in the garden and oven mitts when around the stove to reduce the chance of accidental scrapes and burns. It is important to recognize the early signs of infection: redness, or a sudden increase in pain or swelling. If you notice signs of infection, contact your physician immediately and get a prescription for antibiotics.

Lymphedema can be treated best when it is caught early. This is a source of frustration for physiotherapists who often are not consulted until a woman's edema is in a crisis stage. There are several approaches to the treatment of arm edema: elevation of the affected limb, 'pump' therapy, and support garments.

Arm elevation

Elevating the arm helps the fluid to drain 'downhill.' All you need to do is position the wrist and elbow higher than the shoulder; any higher elevation is not necessary. Think about your arm position from time to time during the day. For example, after having been up and about for two hours, sit and elevate the arm for half an hour, or if travelling, try to get a window seat on the affected side where it is easier to prop up your arm.

Pump therapy

This involves the use of a special multiple chamber air-bag sleeve that helps squeeze the fluid from the hand and arm toward the body. The affected arm is placed inside the sleeve, and the air bags within the sleeve are inflated with compressed air. The pressure can be varied to provide a massaging action which gradually moves the fluid toward the body. The length and number of pumping sessions will depend on the severity of the edema and how successfully the pumping reduces the swelling. Your physiotherapist will carefully measure your arm in several places to monitor the improvement.

Women who have 'soft' edema which indents (or 'pits') when pressed with a finger have the best success with pump therapy. Swelling that feels hard is unlikely to be improved by pumping, but may improve with a combination of treatments which may include laser and pump therapy.

Before starting pump therapy, any infection or cancer recurrence should be treated. Women with only one kidney, limited kidney function or problems with heart failure should begin pump treatments very cautiously because a successful pump session may push several liters of fluid from the arm into the blood circulation.

Compression support garments

Compression support garments consist of elasticized gloves or sleeves that provide external pressure that helps keep the size of the arm small after a session of pump therapy. The external pressure also helps the lymphatic fluid to continue flowing in the arm. The support garments are put on as soon as the pumping session is over. Some women wear their support garment all the time, and others use it only when they are doing sports or other activities that require frequent, repetitive swinging of the arm.

Often, individuals are fitted satisfactorily with a ready-made garment. These are available through physiotherapy clinics or medical supply agents. Alternatively, a custom designed and manufactured garment (Juzo Corporation, Zimmer Co., Ohio, USA) can be made. Your physiotherapist should be able to supply you with more information.

Controlling pain

Easing pain caused by muscle spasms

This is discussed earlier in this chapter.

Controlling pain from trapped nerves

Another cause of pain that is easily treated is subcutaneous nerve entrapment. Nerves under the skin (subcutaneous nerves) can become 'caught' in newly forming tissues as the body heals after surgery or radiation. If there are no metastases in the area then laser treatment is very effective.

Controlling pain from a rotated spine

Pain from a rotated spine is related to shoulder stiffness that occurs after the surgery. When the shoulder muscles are stiff the mid-back works overtime, extending and twisting to raise the arm without the usual help from the shoulder muscles. This can cause the postural malalignment in the spine. When this occurs, many women experience difficulty breathing or have sharp chest pains running from under the shoulder blades to the front of the chest. The pain can come on suddenly and is often longstanding. The pain results when the rotated spine interferes with the usual up-and-out movement of the rib cage. If the physical therapist determines that the spine is rotated, the pain may be corrected by manual therapy and the spine held in place by strengthened muscle developed through a correct exercise program.

Controlling debilitating pain

Pain can be an important warning signal to prevent injury or overuse. However, pain that is debilitating, preventing a woman from 'functioning' and reducing her coping level must be treated. One form of treatment is 'transcutaneous electrical nerve stimulation' (TENS) which acts as an electronic 'nerve block.' This is a portable machine that can be used at home on a daily basis as well as in the clinic.

Hobbies and exercise after surgery
involving removal of lymph nodes

- **Gardening:** Sit on a stool and use hand tools. This prevents overuse of the shoulder and chest muscles (a low stool should be used to prevent upper back strain). Don't lift or hold heavy bags of dirt on your affected side. Be sure to wear a glove!

- **Walking:** When beginning, alternate 15 minutes with your arms at your sides and 15 minutes with your hands in your pockets. No power walking.

- **Swimming:** Begin with a slow front crawl. Gradually work up to more and faster lengths; use caution with the breast stroke and the butterfly.

- **Tennis:** Begin with racquet exercises at home. Bounce the ball on your racquet 10 to 100 times.

- **Aerobics classes (fitness):** Attending more classes is NOT better. If you attend three to four times each week, maintain this program. A switch from no-bounce aerobics to step aerobics will ensure a good work-out without a heavy reliance on the arms and shoulders.

- **Golf:** Begin with putting, the short game irons, then finally work up to your woods. At the driving range, use only one bucket to begin with!

- **Skiing downhill:** Ski packed runs — no ice, hard pack or moguls to begin. Ski deep powder last.

- **Skiing cross-country:** Due to the arm and shoulder action, wearing a support garment is advised.

- **Weight-training:** Use free weights and light hydraulic weights, then increase the weight very gradually.

- **Kayaking:** This is beneficial for strengthening the arm, shoulder and back and reducing arm edema.

- **Canoeing:** Use caution and do short trips. Wear a support garment for long trips.

- **Windsurfing, waterskiing, sailing:** Caution and a support garment must be used due to the amount of arm strain inherent in these sports.

If you have questions about exercising or increasing your daily activities, ask your physiotherapist.

Exercises to speed recovery

The upper back

Exercises that move the shoulders and ribs also move the upper (thoracic) vertebrae, the part of the spine between the shoulder blades. To begin, sit in a comfortable chair with a back-rest that reaches up to the middle of your shoulder blades. You can also place your feet on a low foot stool. This position protects your lower back and neck from overstretching. Do the exercises slowly while breathing deeply to fully expand the ribs.

All exercises begin in the sitting position. Later they can be done standing.

1. Place one arm across the body and breathe out; swing your arm out from your body, raise it upwards and breathe in. Repeat with the other arm. Work both arms equally.

2. Starting with the shoulder, slowly rotate each clockwise, then counter-clockwise.

3. Bend your arms across your chest. Stretch one arm across your chest and touch your fingers behind the opposite shoulder. Repeat on the opposite side.

The arm and shoulder

Exercises for the arm and shoulder involve combinations of bending, stretching and rotation to exercise the joints. Although only one arm may be affected, exercising both arms is important to establish postural balance and to strengthen both arms.

Sitting with your spine stable against the back of the chair:

1. Place your right finger tips on the right shoulder and move the elbow forward and then backwards a few times. Repeat with the other arm.

2. Swing your arms out sideways, then straight up, then pointing forward and down.

3. Swing your arms out forward, straight upward, out sideways and down.

4. Rotate your arms in circles: clockwise, then counter-clockwise.

Shoulder stretches

Stand in a doorway and, placing your hand lightly on the door frame, slide your hand upward. This decreases the strain on the lower back and encourages a long stretch.

CHAPTER THIRTY-FOUR

Reconstructive surgery
by Richard Warren, MD

Should I or shouldn't I?

ALTHOUGH TODAY MORE WOMEN opt for breast reconstruction
than ever before, most women still choose not to have it done
— they are so happy to be rid of their cancer that they cannot
imagine going through any more surgery. For other women,
however, wearing an external prosthesis (see p. 122) is inadequate, impractical and a nuisance, and reconstruction is an
attractive option. The most common reason for breast reconstruction is the psychological desire to correct an obvious deformity and to try to be 'whole' again. For these women, the aim is
to feel as close to normal as possible, which helps to restore
their self-image and self-confidence.

Although most mastectomy patients are potential candidates
for some sort of surgical reconstruction, some are not. Women
in poor health are often not strong enough to undergo the
surgery, and women with advanced breast cancer generally are
not advised to have reconstructive surgery because of cancer-
related medical problems and a poor prognosis from the cancer
itself.

Finally, some women are emotionally not ready to accept
more surgery, with its related risks and complications. Some
women may be coerced into seeking reconstructive surgery by

other individuals in their lives. In the end, the patient seeking breast reconstruction should be physically and mentally healthy, should understand all the facts, and should be doing it for her own reasons, not to please someone else.

Breast cancer treatment always takes precedence

The first goal of breast reconstruction is to not interfere with the treatment of the breast cancer. A plastic surgeon may be consulted before the breast cancer surgery, and may do the reconstruction at the time of a mastectomy. The breast cancer surgeon, plastic surgeon and oncologist should ensure that the cancer treatment is not adversely affected by the reconstruction program.

The first visit to the plastic surgeon

The initial referral to a plastic surgeon is usually arranged by the patient's breast surgeon, family physician or her oncologist. The patient will be asked questions about her expectations, desires, and general health, and a brief physical examination will be done. The patient should ask questions to understand the options available, the proposed surgical procedure, the degree of pain involved, the recovery time, and the risks. She should expect the surgeon to provide diagrams and photographs or introductions to other patients so that she can have a realistic sense of the possible results, which are never perfect. Breast reconstruction is an inexact science, and while every surgeon has produced excellent results, he or she will also have produced unsatisfactory results, and many average results.

Factors that affect the choice of reconstructive procedure

Reconstruction is designed to correct defects left by surgery. The type of procedure recommended will depend largely on the extent of the breast cancer surgery (see Chapter 19), but other factors also influence the choice of procedure and the cosmetic result. These differ from one woman to another and include the amount and looseness of the skin, the direction and length of the original surgical scar, the amount of fat under the skin, the possibility of skin changes caused by radiotherapy, and the shape and size of the other breast.

Surgical techniques

There are a variety of reconstruction techniques; no single technique is right for everyone. The choice of method will depend on the combination of the woman's wishes, the surgeon's preference, the type and extent of deformity, and the nature of the opposite breast. The various possibilities are outlined below in order of increasing complexity.

Implants

The simplest method of reconstruction is the insertion of a breast implant at the site of the original breast. This can be done either at the time of the mastectomy or any time later. This technique is most appropriate for patients who have enough of their own tissue remaining to cover the implant adequately, and for whom the implant alone will match the appearance of the other breast. Breast implants can be inserted in patients who have undergone a partial, a simple, or a modified radical mastectomy.

The implant is placed either through the old incision, or through a new one, against the ribs, tucked underneath the pectoralis muscle. Because the muscle has to be present, this method is not appropriate for reconstruction after a radical mastectomy. The surgery is done under general anesthetic and usually involves a brief hospitalization. Postoperatively, there may be drains in place to remove any fluid build-up, and there will be more pain than from the original mastectomy. Possible problems include an infection, bleeding or problems related to the implant itself, which are discussed further on in this chapter.

Tissue expander

A tissue expander is a device that looks like an empty plastic bag with an attached valve. As with the implant, it is placed behind the pectoralis muscle, but it is then inflated using a small amount of saline (salt water). The idea is that after the surgical site has healed, the bag can be enlarged gradually by injecting salt water into the valve once or twice a week. Like the abdominal skin during pregnancy, the skin of the chest will stretch as the 'pseudo-breast' enlarges. Usually, this process goes on for one or two months in order to overstretch the skin to a size larger than a normal breast. Then, a second operation is done to remove the expander and replace it with a permanent breast implant (Figure 32).

This technique is appropriate for women who don't have enough breast tissue remaining to allow insertion of an implant large enough to match the other breast. Many surgeons who use

Figure 32: The result of breast and nipple reconstruction of both breasts. Tissue expanders were used to stretch the skin from the preoperative stage (upper) until there was sufficient room for the implants to be inserted. At a later operation the nipples were reconstructed (lower).

this technique believe that by overstretching the skin, there will be more of a natural droop to the breast after placement of the permanent implant.

Complications of this technique are the same as for the simple insertion of an implant. The one clear disadvantage of this method is that it involves two operations and many visits to a doctor's office for the fluid injections.

The problem of capsular contracture

By far the most common problem with all breast implants and tissue expanders is the phenomenon of 'capsular contracture' in which a layer of scar tissue forms about the implant and squeezes it into a firm ball. Approximately one-third of all patients experience some form of this, and some are correctable with further surgery. Other problems include bleeding, infection, nerve damage, and with saline implants, the potential of a leak leading to deflation and the necessity of replacing the implant with a new one.

Myocutaneous flaps

A third type of reconstruction involves the use of 'myocutaneous flaps.' This requires the movement of a piece of tissue which includes skin, fat and muscle from one part of the body to another.

The rationale for the use of myocutaneous flaps is that by using the body's own tissue, a more natural-feeling breast may be created, avoiding the complications related to implants. However, there is a trade-off, since the more complex surgery involves increased risks, scarring and recovery time.

In one type of myocutaneous flap operation, the latissimus dorsi muscle (the large triangular muscle from the back) along with the overlying skin, is moved into the mastectomy area. For some women, enough tissue can be transferred from the back to create a good breast size. However, this operation leaves a long scar on the back and eliminates the latissimus as a functioning muscle in the back. Surprisingly, most patients are not aware of this lost function afterwards. The hospital stay is approximately one week.

Currently, the most commonly used flap technique is the 'Transverse Rectus Abdominis Muscle flap,' known as the TRAM flap. This method uses a large section of skin and fat from the lower abdomen along with one or two abdominal muscles. A breast mound is fashioned out of the skin and fat which has been brought up from the abdomen. Often, the abdominal muscle layer will not close easily, and a synthetic mesh must be sutured into place to prevent an abdominal hernia. Postoperatively, the patient has considerable discomfort in the abdominal area. Drains will be present at the breast site, as well as in the abdomen, and hospitalization will be about a week.

Although using the body's own tissues sounds attractive, this is a complex method of breast reconstruction, with additional possible complications including abdominal wall hernia, part of the flap not survivng, thrombophlebitis (formation of blood clots in the veins), and postoperative lung problems.

Nipple reconstruction

Many women who seek breast reconstruction are happy once a breast mound has been created because they have achieved their objective of looking good in clothes and not having to use an external prosthesis. Other women wish to go further and choose to undergo another operation to create a nipple. Both the central nipple and the surrounding areola need to be created from grafts of tissue from other parts of the body. For example, the more darkly pigmented areola can be fashioned from a portion of the opposite areola or a skin graft from high on the inside of the thigh. The color match can be improved by tattooing the skin graft (Figure 32).

Nipple-areola reconstruction is relatively minor surgery, with the main problems relating to partial graft failure and mismatched color.

Matching the breasts exactly

Paradoxically, the easiest situation for achieving identical-looking breasts (symmetry) with mastectomy reconstruction is when both breasts are reconstructed (Figure 32). Although the goal of reconstructing one breast is to match the normal breast, an exact match is never really possible. To get a close match, the normal breast may need to be altered. This may require breast uplift (mastopexy) or breast reduction. Both of these procedures create extensive scars on the normal breast, and introduce new risks and complications to the procedure.

Are breast implants dangerous?

Over the years a number of different materials have been tried for reconstructing breasts, including sponges, human fat, injected substances, and breast implants. Other than the use of the patient's own tissue, such as with the TRAM flap, only breast implants have been successful. However, their use has become controversial. Invented in the 1960s, breast implants have been manufactured in many forms, the basic design being a bag of silicone rubber filled with some sort of soft material. The most widely used type has been one filled with a silicone liquid or a gel, while another type is filled with salt water (saline). A third type of implant was the 'bi-lumen,' a hybrid type consisting of silicone gel surrounded by a second bag of saline.

In recent years it has become apparent that implants filled with silicone gel leak microscopic amounts of silicone over time, and there have been reports of health problems, mainly autoimmune diseases such as arthritis, possibly related to the silicone gel. At present, extensive studies are being done to determine the validity of these concerns, but the absolute risk of these complications appears to be very small. Nevertheless, health authorities in the United States and Canada have taken the safest position, deciding to remove silicone gel implants from the marketplace in 1991. In the United States, silicone gel-filled implants are still available under certain circumstances and on special request. There does not appear to be any need to remove a silicone gel prosthesis if it is not causing the woman any problems.

The standard implant used in North America today is the saline-filled breast implant. Saline implants are considered safe because a leak will only release salt water, which is the same as the major fluid component of our blood. This means that if the fluid leaks it is readily absorbed by the body without any health risk other than the need to replace the implant.

Timing of breast reconstruction

Traditionally, breast reconstruction after mastectomy was delayed for a period of time, often a year, to allow time to complete additional therapies such as radiation and chemotherapy, and to allow the woman to recover mentally and physically from her ordeal before she proceeded with more extensive surgery. This wait is no longer thought to be necessary and some patients now undergo immediate reconstruction. The reconstruction procedure is done at the same time as the mastectomy. Advantages of this include reducing the number of operations and avoiding the trauma of seeing a completely denuded mastectomy site. Also, some procedures such as the free TRAM flap are easier if done at the time of the mastectomy.

Disadvantages of immediate reconstruction include the coordination of two surgeons, a long operation (six or more hours) and an increased risk of complications. Some oncologists prefer that additional therapies such as chemotherapy and radiation be done without an implant in place. Furthermore, some patients who may have felt that they wanted reconstruction become used to their mastectomy and do not seek reconstruction at all. Timing, then, is a decision that should be made in consultation with everyone involved.

SECTION THIRTEEN

Life Style Issues

CHAPTER THIRTY-FIVE

Diet and vitamins

by Shirley Hobenshield, RDN

WE EAT TO SATISFY a complex set of needs — emotional, cultural, sensual and, of course, nutritional. Eating well, in every sense of the word, is one of the most supportive things that a woman with breast cancer can do for herself. Regardless of your situation, choosing a healthy diet can help you to feel as well as possible.

What is a healthy diet?

Healthy eating does not mean following a rigid diet with hard and fast rules about good and bad foods. It simply means emphasizing certain types of food while still enjoying the pleasures of eating well. In North America we tend to eat too much fat and not enough fruits, vegetables and whole grains. However, changing our diet to a healthy one does not mean banishing all high fat foods like French fries or chocolate cake. It simply means changing the focus, for example, enjoying a bowl of whole grain cereal instead of a doughnut for breakfast, or having fresh fruit for dessert more often than cake or pastry.

A healthy diet also means achieving balance, that is, eating foods in the right proportions to make sure that protein, vitamin and mineral needs are being met. The Box on p. 214 gives a broad outline of the categories of foods that should be included in a balanced diet.

Recommended foods

In one day you should eat:

5 to 12 servings of grain products
5 to 10 servings of vegetables and fruit
2 to 4 servings of milk products
2 to 3 servings of meat and alternatives

Grain products (each is 1 serving)
- 1 slice of bread
- $\frac{1}{2}$ a bagel or pita bread
- $\frac{1}{2}$ cup (125 mL) of cooked pasta or rice
- $\frac{3}{4}$ cup (175 grams) of cooked cereal
- 30 grams of dry cereal ($\frac{1}{3}$ to 1 cup, depending on the type of cereal)

Vegetables and fruit (each is 1 serving)
- 1 medium-sized vegetable or fruit, such as one carrot, potato, apple, orange or banana
- $\frac{1}{2}$ cup (125 mL) of vegetables or fruit, such as corn, broccoli, berries, peas, or applesauce
- 1 cup (250 mL) of salad or $\frac{1}{2}$ cup (125 mL) of juice

Milk products (each is 1 serving)
- 1 cup (250 mL) of milk
- $\frac{3}{4}$ cup (175 mL) of yogurt
- 2 ounces (60 grams) of cheese
- $\frac{1}{2}$ cup (125 mL) of high-protein milk*

Meat and alternatives (each is 1 serving)
- 2 ounces (60 grams) or $\frac{1}{2}$ cup chicken, fish or meat
- $\frac{1}{2}$ cup (125 mL) cooked legumes, e.g. kidney beans, lentils
- 1 to 1$\frac{1}{2}$ cups (250 to 375 mL) soya yogurt
- $\frac{1}{2}$ cup (125 mL) cottage cheese
- $\frac{1}{2}$ cup (125 mL) firm tofu
- 2 eggs
- 2 cups (500 mL) soya drink
- 3 tablespoons (45 mL) peanut butter
- 5 tablespoons (75 mL) almond, cashew or sesame butter

* High protein milk — mix 1 cup (250 mL) of fluid milk with $\frac{1}{4}$ cup (60 mL) of skim milk powder. Use as a base for soups, puddings and hot or cold drinks.

Is there a link between diet and breast cancer?

In the last few years people have been studying this idea. However, because no firm evidence has turned up as yet, the most reasonable diet to follow is the one that gives you the best overall health. For most people this means less fat and more fruits, vegetables and fiber.

Part of the problem in studying the link between diet and cancer is that there are so many other factors involved such as environmental causes and heredity.

Is there a special diet to follow while undergoing breast cancer therapy?

You should follow a normal healthy diet, but with a twist. Your body needs extra protein to help healing after surgery or while going through chemotherapy or radiation therapy. Protein is found in foods such as meat, fish and chicken, milk products and eggs. A more complete list is shown in the Box. You should aim to eat at least two servings of meat (or an alternative) and two servings of milk products each day.

If you're taking chemotherapy

During chemotherapy, nausea, a sore mouth, taste changes and mild diarrhea may occur.

Ease nausea with starchy snacks and light drinks

Nausea is best controlled by a combination of medications and certain foods. Dry, starchy foods like crackers and dry cereals, nibbled often, can help minimize that empty stomach feeling that can make nausea worse. Fluids like flat ginger ale, weak tea, diluted fruit juice or just plain ice water are generally better tolerated than milk shakes, coffee or very sweet juices. Keeping a thermos or giant cup close by can help remind you of the importance of drinking lots of fluid during chemotherapy.

If the smell of cooking food makes nausea worse, try to avoid being in the kitchen if possible. If this is not realistic, it's a good idea to stock up on purchased or homemade frozen dinners, such as stews, that can be easily reheated.

Soothe mouth sores

If mouth sores occur during chemotherapy, certain foods should be avoided until the sores heal, such as oranges and grapefruit, salty or spicy foods, or rough foods, like toast. Many women find frozen yogurt, ice milk and other cool foods very soothing.

If foods taste different

Some women notice that certain foods taste different during chemotherapy. For example, meat may taste bitter or metallic. If this happens, choose more bland, high protein foods like eggs, milk or tofu to make eating more enjoyable. Food cravings may also occur. For instance, one woman craved chicken and ate it three times a day during treatment. Many women report that fruits and certain vegetables are often the most appealing foods.

If you have diarrhea or gas

Mild diarrhea and gas can be a problem. You can minimize diarrhea by limiting your intake of bowel stimulants like alcohol and caffeine, and eating less high fiber foods. Excess gas can be at least partially controlled by eating less gas-forming foods like legumes, cabbage, brussel sprouts, melons, apples and grapes.

If you're taking radiation therapy

Most women undergoing radiation therapy for breast cancer report very little disturbance in their usual eating habits. However, treatment-induced fatigue can make food preparation more of a chore than usual. It's a good idea to have on hand a variety of convenience foods like frozen dinners. Meals can be simple but still nutritious — a sandwich or a bowl of cereal with milk and fruit may be fine. Women whose radiation treatment involves the throat area can develop temporary soreness and a feeling of a lump or discomfort during swallowing. Eating soft, moist foods is helpful, such as poached eggs, creamed fish, chicken stew or fruit yogurt. An even smoother consistency can be achieved by putting foods through a blender. Very hot foods such as tea or soup can make a sore throat worse.

What about gaining weight during treatment?

Regardless of the type of treatment you are receiving, unwanted weight gain is quite frequent. The exact cause is unclear, but it may be due to a number of factors, including decreased physical activity, eating frequently to control nausea, eating as an antidote to boredom or psychological distress, or because of an increased appetite if you recently quit smoking.

How can weight gain be controlled?

It's not a good idea to try to lose weight during treatment because it puts unnecessary stress on the body and can actually slow down healing. A better goal is to maintain your weight until treatment is complete. You can do this by limiting high fat foods and eating more fruits, vegetables and whole grains. If frequent eating is necessary to control nausea, low fat foods are a good choice, like crackers, cereal and skim milk, bread and jam, and canned soft fruits. Women who are taking the hormone treatment megestrol acetate (Megace®) may find weight control especially difficult, but a healthy, low fat, high fiber diet can help.

Are extra vitamins and minerals helpful during treatment?

Daily supplements

If you find it difficult to eat a variety of vegetables, fruits and whole grain foods, then a daily multivitamin/mineral tablet is recommended.

Large doses

It's not yet clear whether the use of large doses of vitamins and minerals help in cancer treatment. Those who support their use point out that since cancer treatments can depress the immune system, taking vitamins and minerals could help restore immune function. Although a number of nutrients are required for the immune system to function properly (including vitamins

A, C, E, B$_6$, beta-carotene, folic acid, zinc and iron), too much of a good thing is not necessarily better and can be harmful. For example, too much zinc actually depresses the immune system.

Another theory is that the antioxidant vitamins — vitamins C, E, and beta-carotene — are required to help repair damaged cells. This is being studied, but there's not enough evidence as yet to indicate that large amounts of these vitamins do help in cancer treatment. Green and yellow vegetables contain moderate amounts of vitamins C and beta-carotene. These vegetables are part of healthy eating but there is not enough data to support taking 'megadoses' at this time. Women who consume huge amounts of carrots daily will notice that their skin and the 'whites' of their eyes become orange.

If you are interested in using high doses of vitamin or mineral supplements, it is a good idea to discuss this with your physicians to confirm that these supplements can be used safely along with other treatments you may be receiving.

Once treatment's over, keep eating well

Even after treatment is over, it makes sense to continue eating less fat and more fruits, vegetables and whole grain foods. Besides a possible link to breast cancer risk, too much fat in the diet has been linked to heart disease and obesity. By simply becoming aware of where fat is found in your diet, you can take steps to reduce your fat intake. Try to remove visible fats on chicken or meat wherever you can. Also, limit the amount of fat you add to foods by skipping butter or margarine on sandwiches, using light salad dressings, and using extra herbs and spices instead of cream sauces.

Finally, be aware of hidden fat. This is the trickiest — it's found in foods like cookies, cakes, chips, ice cream and cheese. You can limit hidden fat by reading food labels carefully and choosing alternatives such as low fat cheese.

More advice on nutrition

You can obtain further advice about nutrition by contacting a registered dietitian at your regional cancer center or community hospital. As well, in some places there are nutrition hotlines staffed by qualified dietitians. Check with your local dietetic association about nutrition hotlines in your area.

In the United States, the phone number of the Consumer Nutrition Hotline of the American Dietetic Association is 1-800-366-1655. Dial-a-Dietitian in British Columbia can be reached at 1-800-667-DIET.

The Additional Reading section lists several cookbooks devoted to lower fat, higher fiber meals. The recipes are easy to follow and most importantly, taste great!

CHAPTER THIRTY-SIX

Stress and relaxation
by Lis Smith, CCH

What is stress?

STRESS IS WOVEN into the fabric of life. At healthy levels it challenges us and promotes activity, but when you feel 'overloaded' or 'lose control' then the stress level is no longer healthy. The uncertainty and fears surrounding a diagnosis of breast cancer can lead to a feeling of overload just when there is a great need to be 'in control' and it can threaten your well-being.

How much stress am I feeling?

Stress is a subjective response and is not expressed the same way in each person. When stress becomes too great the mind may say that you are 'coping,' but the body gives more accurate signals. If you recognize and acknowledge your own stress response you can begin to deal with it.

To assess your own response to stress, learn to scan your body while asking yourself questions. Start at the top of your head, searching for tightness between the brow and eyes. Are your lips pursed? Is your jaw clenched? Are your shoulders hunched up near your ears? Normally, one doesn't notice doing these things until alerted by a pounding headache or lower back pain at the end of the day caused by holding muscles so tense.

Do you feel a tightness in the throat, a constriction in the chest or a churning stomach? Are you breathing shallowly, using only the upper part of your chest? Does your heart beat fast? Some people notice that their sleep pattern is disturbed, and others eat more than they need because eating is comforting.

When in distress the mind doesn't focus and function the way it usually does. You may forget your own telephone number or an important appointment. Your thoughts may be dark and repetitive, and after only an hour's sleep you may lie awake for hours doing what has been so aptly called 'awfulizing.' Emotionally, you are not as steady as usual, and find yourself in tears over something that you would normally take in stride.

To be told to 'relax' at a time like this may seem unreasonable. You do know, however, that when you are not feeling the effects of an overload of stress, you find yourself filled with a tranquil energy and a sense of control. How do you achieve this elusive feeling, especially after a recent diagnosis of breast cancer?

How can I reduce stress and regain a sense of control?

Reading this book, gaining knowledge about breast cancer, is one practical way to help yourself find that sense of control. Also, finding someone simply to listen is of enormous value.

Research has shown that even twenty minutes a day of relaxation can have a beneficial effect on the body. It doesn't matter whether it is transcendental meditation or simply sitting quietly watching the birds at a feeder outside the window. Twenty minutes of steady walking or other exercise works for some people. Tai-Chi and yoga also use movement to bring the body and mind into a state of harmony. Meditation, in which the mind focuses on a particular word (mantra) or object (mandala), or simply focusing on the rising and falling of the breath stills the chattering mind and restores a sense of equilibrium. Anything that allows the body to be at ease and the mind to quieten a little appears to bring back balance and harmony. Think of the ocean. Even when a storm is raging, deep below there is a place where the water is calm. So it is with your own self. You need to find the way down to that place deep within yourself where you are calm and in control, even in the midst of chaos.

Women are used to being responsible for others and putting their own needs last. Giving yourself permission to take some time for yourself can be an important part of the healing process. Be your own good care-giver; it is okay to say 'yes' to your own needs.

The relaxation response

Relaxation is about tranquil energy and gaining a sense of control so that you can respond to situations and make good choices rather than just react. It is interesting that the ancient Chinese symbol for crisis has two components, one meaning 'danger,' the other meaning 'opportunity.' Gaining a sense of control gives you an opportunity to make creative choices.

The breath is the pulse of the mind. You can slow your racing thoughts simply by changing your breathing, especially by breathing from the bottom of the diaphragm instead of the shallow, tight breathing from high in the chest that usually accompanies stress. For example: take a comfortable, deep breath, hold it to the count of four and then let it out with a sigh. Repeat this four times. Feel how your shoulders release and your facial muscles soften. When you find yourself experiencing tension, remind yourself to take a sighing breath.

'Autogenics' is another way to occupy the thinking mind by getting it busy with repeated words such as 'My right arm is heavy, my right arm is warm.' By this repetition the mind starts to convince the body that its different parts are at ease. This feeling of bodily comfort induces a sense of calm control.

Another way to achieve the relaxation response is to imagine yourself in a beautiful place, perhaps in nature or a delightful room, or to relive the memory of a time of achievement and strength. This is the opposite of 'awfulizing,' as you use your body-mind connection to create sensations of peace and 'connectedness.' Audiotapes can also be very helpful by coaching you through these experiences (see Additional Reading).

'Quick fixes'

Sometimes finding even twenty minutes a day for relaxing seems like a tall order. You may wish to experiment with some 'quick fixes' which will help you become familiar with the healing benefits of relaxation.

Whenever you are particularly stressed you quite naturally do one of these 'quick fixes' already: you sigh. You can cultivate sighing as a way towards relaxation. After three or four comfortable sighing breaths you will find that the muscles of the face are more at ease, the chest feels more open and the shoulders are softer. Because one needs regular reminders to sigh, try putting little colored dots in all sorts of places such as on your steering wheel, on the telephone or on your purse. These dots can serve as triggers, reminders to take a breath, hold it to the count of four and then sigh the breath out. Do this throughout the day.

Another 'quick fix' is to practice a quick progressive muscle relaxation every time you sit down. Let tension flow from the top of your head out through the soles of your feet. Or take a 30-second vacation and recall a beautiful place or happy, carefree time.

Certain fragrances are known to soothe and elevate one's mood. Try a few drops of neroli oil, lavender, geranium or another fragrance which pleases you as you relax in a warm bath. Many health food stores and pharmacies carry aroma therapy products.

Increasingly, you will recognize the importance of your own role in the healing process, in partnership with your physicians and the treatments and medications offered. Learning your role can add a rich dimension to the power of the partnership.

What if Cancer Recurs?

CHAPTER THIRTY-SEVEN

Follow-up and diagnosis of recurrence

OFTEN, IT IS ONLY at the end of treatment that women start to worry about the possibility of a relapse. 'What if the breast cancer recurs? When will it recur? What can I do to prevent it from coming back? What is my prognosis if it does relapse? Will I die? How long have I got?'

What are the chances of a recurrence?

The risk of relapse is related to several factors, including whether the cancer is in situ or invasive, the size of the tumor, the clinical stage, and the presence and number of cancer-involved lymph nodes. Patients with in situ disease have a very low risk of the cancer recurring elsewhere in the body (metastasis), but there is a possibility of local recurrence or of a cancer developing in the other breast.

For invasive cancers, the risk of relapse is related to the clinical stage. In clinical stage I disease (a small tumor and no cancer found in the axillary lymph nodes), 75% to 95% of patients will be alive with no recurrence 10 years or longer after treatment (see Chapter 17 for a description of clinical stages). In more advanced stages the risk of relapse is naturally greater. Approximately 50% of stage II patients and 75% of those with a locally advanced cancer will develop a recurrence either locally or elsewhere in the body in the first five to ten years after treatment.

New therapies are being studied all over the world. Information is shared internationally so that women can gain access to new therapies quickly, hopefully improving these statistics so that over the next few years fewer women will suffer a relapse.

Local recurrence

A local recurrence refers to the area that includes the breast, the armpit, the skin or chest wall, and surrounding lymph nodes. It is important to realize that the cancer may recur on the chest wall after a mastectomy; patients should check this area monthly as part of the breast self-examination.

Radiation to the breast, chest wall and lymph node areas and tamoxifen therapy can significantly reduce the occurrence of relapse in these areas, but it is not clear whether adjuvant chemotherapy reduces local relapse.

Recurrence elsewhere in the body ('distant' or 'systemic')

A distant or systemic recurrence occurs when breast cancer cells travel in the blood stream or lymphatic channels from the breast to other parts of the body. The term for this movement of cancer cells is 'metastasize,' and the new tumor that develops in the new site is called a 'metastasis.' An example is if breast cancer cells travel from the breast to the bone. Breast cancer cells most often metastasize to the bones, liver, lungs, skin, soft tissue, lymph nodes, brain or ovaries. Although most recurrences occur between two and six years after the initial diagnosis (if they occur at all), breast cancer may recur systemically many years later.

When should I suspect a systemic recurrence?

Most systemic recurrences cause symptoms; they are rarely silent. The symptoms depend on which organ is affected. For example, breast cancer that has travelled to the bones will often cause pain, while recurrences in the lungs may cause cough or shortness of breath. It is often difficult for a patient who has recently been diagnosed to know which symptoms might be indicative of recurrent disease and which symptoms are simply normal aches and pains. It takes time for a woman to start trusting her body again after a diagnosis of breast cancer, and the worry about systemic relapse makes it hard to be at ease.

In general, symptoms of recurrence are more persistent than normal aches and pains and become more severe. For example, a backache that's brought on by moving furniture usually feels bad for a day or two and then gradually gets better. Metastatic bone disease in the back may come on gradually, may come and go with activity and may respond to pain killers, but it will not go away completely and stay away. Instead, it will become more persistent. It is very common for women to be more aware of their bodies after a diagnosis of cancer. It is normal to think that an ache, for example in the leg, is due to cancer. However, if a pain comes and goes in 24 hours it is not likely to be cancer and you don't need to worry.

On the other hand, if you are worried about a new symptom, especially if it is persistent or getting worse, you should see your doctor, who can do an examination and order any investigations that may be necessary. If everything is normal and the symptoms continue to bother you, they may be due to something other than the breast cancer. The problem should be pursued, and the doctor may need to do further tests to find the cause. Not all new symptoms mean a recurrence of breast cancer, but they do mean you should see your doctor and have them evaluated.

How should I be followed to detect a recurrence?

All women who have been diagnosed with a breast cancer need follow-up visits to check for a local recurrence or metastasis. However, medical opinion differs on the best follow-up schedule for detecting systemic recurrences, and women's needs also vary. Many women are more comfortable with careful follow-up and the reassurance that there is no detectable recurrence. Other women find the follow-up testing causes unnecessary anxiety, and they would prefer to be investigated only when they experience symptoms. It is important that the woman and her doctor agree on a schedule of follow-up which provides reassurance and detects most recurrences promptly, but allows the woman to return to normal living without feeling like an invalid.

Unfortunately, we must acknowledge that with treatments available today there is very little advantage to the early detection of a systemic recurrence, and most physicians do not recommend performing lots of x-rays and blood tests to look for metastases. The situation is different for local recurrence which may be curable with further local therapy. Also, it is useful to detect the development of a second breast cancer in the opposite breast as early as possible since this too may be curable.

Your responsibilities

You are responsible for some aspects of the follow-up. You need to learn how to do a thorough monthly breast self-examination. This includes examining the uninvolved breast, the radiated breast, or the chest wall if a mastectomy has been done. Any new findings or changes should be reported immediately to a doctor. It's important to know that not all changes are recurrences. Many women develop thickened areas or redness in a radiated breast, or thickened areas along the scar. Often, it is difficult to know if the thickening is cancerous or not, and a biopsy and mammogram may be necessary. You should show your doctor the area of concern and he or she will do a physical examination and order additional tests if necessary.

Six-month visits

After completing your initial treatment for cancer, you should be seen by a doctor at least every six months for a careful examination of the breasts, chest wall and lymph nodes as well as lungs, liver and abdomen. You should mention any new symptoms such as bony aches and pains, cough or shortness of breath, nausea and weight loss, or new lumps and bumps, since these may be indications of recurrent disease.

Blood tests are often normal despite evidence of a local or even systemic recurrence. However, some physicians recommend blood tests every six months or so to check liver enzymes and tumor marker tests. These are usually not necessary in a low-risk, well patient, but may be recommended for women with a higher risk of relapse and for women with symptoms. Routine bone or liver scans are not recommended in women with no symptoms. Chest x-rays should be done if there are any symptoms that relate to the lungs, or at the discretion of the doctor in a high-risk patient.

Mammograms

We recommend mammograms of the irradiated breast every six to twelve months to detect any small abnormalities that may develop. It is important to state that not all mammogram abnormalities are cancer. After radiation and surgery there may be changes in the breast such as scarring or swelling which is often monitored most effectively with regular mammograms. Mammograms of the unaffected breast should also be performed once a year.

CHAPTER THIRTY-EIGHT

Treatment of
a local recurrence

WHEN THE CANCER RECURS at or near the site of the original breast cancer many patients are surprised and confused. How can the cancer recur after surgery, radiation and chemotherapy? There are a number of theories, including: 1) that cancer cells are left in the skin after surgery, 2) that cancer cells remain in the muscles or lymphatic system of the chest wall after surgery in an area that was not removed with a mastectomy or partial mastectomy, and 3) that the cancer cells were present in the blood stream before the operation and returned to the chest wall after the surgery. Each of these theories may in some cases be correct, but it is usually impossible to know why the cancer recurred in a particular case.

How are local recurrences treated?

Local relapses often require local treatments such as surgery or radiation, especially if no other recurrence is detected elsewhere in the body. However, in other cases, if there is a high risk of the cancer recurring elsewhere in the near future, then the local recurrence may be better treated with systemic treatment such as chemotherapy or hormones.

Studies have been done to determine whether chemotherapy added to surgery and/or radiation will cure more women with local relapse than surgery and/or radiation alone. Although these trials have not yet shown a definite benefit of adding chemotherapy, if the woman is young and has not had previous chemotherapy, it may be recommended after the local recurrence has been removed.

Can the cancer recur in a breast after partial mastectomy and radiation?

Yes, cancer recurs in a breast after radiation and conservative surgery in approximately 10% of women treated with this combination. This type of local relapse is a special situation that can often be treated successfully but usually requires a mastectomy. A recurrence in the breast after a partial mastectomy and radiation has a better prognosis than a local recurrence on the chest wall after a mastectomy, and is often not associated with any other relapse. To detect a small, curable recurrence we recommend physical examinations and mammography every six to twelve months for five years and annually thereafter.

Treatment of a recurrence in the breast

The treatment for a local recurrence in a breast with a previous partial mastectomy and radiation is generally a total mastectomy. The reason that the lump alone cannot be removed is that the rest of the breast is still at risk of developing cancer and further radiation cannot be given again. Although hormone therapy (usually tamoxifen) or even chemotherapy may be recommended following surgical treatment, the benefit of these treatments is not yet clear.

Treatment of a local recurrence after mastectomy

Recurrence of breast cancer may occur on the chest wall, or in lymph glands in the armpit (axilla), above the collar bone (supraclavicular fossa) or behind the breast bone (internal mammary nodes). If the patient has not previously received radiation then the usual treatment is to remove the recurrence surgically (if it is small and localized) and then give radiation therapy (see Chapter 25). If the recurrence is very extensive or cancer recurs within the chest wall and lymph glands after previous radiation therapy, treatment needs to be individualized. However, in these situations the usual approach is to use hormones or chemotherapy.

CHAPTER THIRTY-NINE

Treatment of recurrence elsewhere in the body (metastasis)

Why does the cancer recur elsewhere?

CANCER COMES BACK elsewhere in the body (a 'systemic recurrence') when breast cancer cells that were already outside the breast at the time of the initial diagnosis were not caught during the first treatment. Although adjuvant chemotherapy or hormone therapy is given to try to destroy these cells, it is not always effective. Cells that are resistant to the drugs are not killed and may divide and grow into detectable cancer metastases. Unfortunately, cancer also recurs in some women who were initially thought to be at low risk of a relapse.

What can I expect if I have a recurrence elsewhere?

The behavior of the returning cancer seems to depend on a number of factors, including:

a) the amount of time passed since the original cancer was diagnosed: the more time in between the better the outcome
b) the type of cancer: the less aggressive, the better
c) the tumor's estrogen receptor status: estrogen receptor-positive tumors respond better to treatment than estrogen receptor-negative tumors

d) the number of tumor sites: the fewer, the better; and
e) the sites of the metastases: for example, bone metastases are often slower growing than liver metastases.

The most important factor, however, is how the cancer responds to therapy. If the cancer responds to one type of treatment, then it is more likely that other treatments will also be effective in controlling it. If the cancer does not shrink in response to any of the usual treatments, the outlook is not as good.

What are the goals of treatment?

The goals of treatment of metastatic breast cancer are to relieve symptoms, maintain quality of life, and prolong survival. The word 'cure' comes up with hopes for a successful treatment of the systemic recurrence. However, disappointment often follows when the physician cannot guarantee or even predict promising results. Many people live with longstanding (chronic) diseases that cannot be cured, such as heart disease, emphysema, diabetes, and arthritis, in which treatment is not curative but is given to avoid severe complications and symptoms. Metastatic breast cancer can be similar to one of these chronic diseases, with a series of treatments given to decrease the symptoms and avoid complications. After a systemic recurrence, breast cancer is usually not curable. However, the length of life can be as much as ten years or more, and it is impossible to predict how long a particular individual may survive.

The treatments

Patients with metastatic breast cancer usually receive a variety of treatments, including hormones, radiotherapy, chemotherapy, nutritional support, pain management, psychological support, and sometimes surgery. Even after a diagnosis of recurrence is made, the best treatment for a woman with *no symptoms* may be *no treatment* until symptoms occur. This is because a treatment may have side effects that are worse than the disease.

Judging whether to give treatment is sometimes a delicate balance. A metastatic tumor may simply be watched for a month or two (if it is not causing problems) to chart how quickly it is growing.

Systemic (whole body) therapy with hormones or chemotherapy should be given if there is widespread symptomatic cancer, if the cancer seems to be growing rapidly, or if there is widespread involvement of organs that is impairing their function.

The type of systemic therapy initially used depends on a number of factors:

a) the type of the original tumor: whether it was estrogen receptor-positive

b) the length of time since the original diagnosis: a long period of time despite an initial estrogen receptor-negative tumor may suggest a hormone-responsive cancer

c) the organs involved: bone metastases may respond better to hormones

d) the severity of the symptoms: with widespread cancer in the lungs the patient cannot wait until the tumor responds to hormone therapy, and

e) the age of the patient: chemotherapy may be too harsh for an elderly woman with other health problems.

When is hormone therapy used?

For most systemic recurrences the first therapy used is hormones. Even if the original cancer was an estrogen receptor-negative tumor, if a few years have passed since that diagnosis, the cancer may respond. However, if the cancer is growing rapidly in vital organs such as the lungs or liver, hormones may not be the best treatment because they often take a couple of months to show an effect, and the cancer may be causing severe problems by then. The therapies with the fewest side effects are used first, followed by ones that are less well tolerated. This approach is used to maintain an optimal quality of life. Unfortunately, even if there is a good response to a particular hormone, the response does not last forever. Other hormone drugs may then be tried until the cancer either no longer responds or is growing rapidly in a vital organ such as the liver or lungs.

Postmenopausal women

For postmenopausal women, tamoxifen is usually the first treatment. If the cancer recurs a few years after adjuvant tamoxifen has been discontinued, the recurrence may respond to another course of this hormone. However, if the cancer recurs very soon after completion of the adjuvant treatment, there is less chance of seeing a response to tamoxifen.

Premenopausal women

For premenopausal women the initial hormone treatment can be either tamoxifen or reduction of estrogen by surgical removal of the ovaries or radiation of the ovaries. (Removing the ovaries from postmenopausal women is of no value since they are no longer producing estrogens.) A new medication, Zoladex®, also works by stopping the production of estrogen in the ovaries.

For how long can hormone therapy be used?

As mentioned above, hormone therapy is usually continued until the recurrent cancer no longer responds. Most oncologists try one or two hormones before deciding whether the tumor is responding or not. All hormones act slowly, so the tumor's response can't be assessed before six to twelve weeks, although the patient may begin to feel better before that. Since the hormones are used in order of increasing side effects, many clinics start with tamoxifen, and then follow with megestrol, aminoglutethimide, fluoxymesterone, and medroxyprogesterone.

When is chemotherapy used?

Chemotherapy is used as the first treatment for a systemic recurrence when the tumor is not likely to respond to hormones. This may include a fast-growing tumor, one that occurs soon after the initial diagnosis, or an estrogen receptor-negative cancer. Chemotherapy is also used to treat cancers that have not responded to a trial of hormone therapy or those which initially responded but are no longer doing so.

How is an appropriate drug combination chosen?

The choice of drugs to treat the metastatic cancer depends on previous treatment that the woman has had and the amount of time between any adjuvant chemotherapy and the recurrence. Drugs may be given individually or in combinations with other drugs. If a woman has had no previous chemotherapy, the most effective drug combination usually consists of doxorubicin (Adriamycin®), cyclophosphamide and 5-fluorouracil. If the patient is elderly or has a significant heart problem, doxorubicin is not usually used. If adjuvant chemotherapy was given, but more than a year before the recurrence, the same drugs may be used as before, possibly in a new combination.

If the patient has had adjuvant therapy recently, the initial treatment for the metastatic cancer may be a new drug, the recently studied paclitaxel (Taxol®). This drug has shown promising results in some women, with tumors shrinking and symptoms decreasing. Combinations of other drugs, including mitoxantrone (Novantrone®), mitomycin C, methotrexate, epirubicin, vinblastine, cisplatinum and thiotepa also may be used. These drugs, if given in a different schedule or by a different route, may bring about another response. For example, 5-fluorouracil given as a slow, continuous intravenous infusion over six weeks may bring about a response from a tumor that did not respond to intermittent doses of the drug given once every three weeks. Newer agents such as vinorelbine (Navelbine®) and docetaxel (Taxotere®) are also being studied.

For how long is chemotherapy continued?

Chemotherapy may be given for a set number of courses or may be continued for as long as there is evidence of response. Different treatment centers may have different policies. If there is a good response to chemotherapy, a second type of chemotherapy may be tried when the cancer recurs. If the cancer does not respond to two different types of chemotherapy, it may be a very stubborn and resistant cancer. In this situation the oncologist may decide to avoid further chemotherapy if it is causing side effects and not benefitting the patient.

Often, chemotherapy can effectively decrease the symptoms of metastatic cancer, such as the shortness of breath that may occur if the cancer is in the lungs. It can also reduce bone aches, enlarged lymph nodes, tumors of the skin or liver, or tumors in the abdomen. Unfortunately it can rarely overcome the fatigue that is a common complaint of women with recurrent cancer.

Studies are evaluating high-dose chemotherapy and bone marrow transplants as treatments for women with systemic recurrences, but this has not been shown to be a better treatment.

When is radiation used to treat systemic recurrences?

Radiation can be given for recurrent tumors that cause symptoms in a specific area of the body. This includes recurrent tumors in the lymph nodes in the chest that cause shortness of breath, tumors near the esophagus that interfere with swallowing, or tumors in the bones, brain and other structures.

The decision to treat with radiation is based on several factors: the site of the recurrence, the symptoms that may be relieved by the treatment, the symptoms that may be caused by the treatment, and how much radiation the area has received in the past. Different organs in the body can tolerate different doses of radiation before the side effects become too severe. Some areas can only be treated once with radiation, while other areas can be retreated.

Radiation can be given either at the same time as hormones or chemotherapy, or by itself. Radiation often decreases pain very successfully, particularly bone pain, and prevents further bone damage caused by the cancer. The relief from pain occurs because radiation kills cancer cells, causing tumors to shrink and pressure in the bones to be relieved. The pain relief may be immediate or gradual over a month or so. Bones tolerate higher doses of radiation than many other tissues, so depending on the doses used, a bone can sometimes be treated with radiation more than once.

If the cancer recurs in the chest wall, radiation may be used to treat the recurrence even if there is also evidence of cancer elsewhere in the body. Various types of radiation can be used for recurrences on or under the skin, depending on how deep the metastases are and how much radiation has been given before.

The mainstay of treatment for a cancer that recurs in the brain is radiation treatment of the brain to shrink the cancer. The side effects of the therapy may include fatigue, mild nausea and headaches. Hair loss always occurs when the whole brain is treated with radiation, but it begins to grow back after three or four months.

Is surgery ever used to treat systemic recurrences?

Yes, sometimes. If there are bone metastases, surgery may be used to stabilize the bone to avoid fractures, or to mend bones that have already fractured. Pins or plates can be used to decrease the pain by making the bone more stable. Occasionally, surgery may be used to remove a lump or recurrence on the skin even when there is evidence of other metastases.

If the woman is in reasonable overall shape and has only one site of metastatic disease, surgery can be used to remove it from the lungs, liver or brain, especially in cases of slow-growing tumors. With breast cancer, however, it is rare to have just a single metastasis, so very few patients are considered for this treatment. Since the cancer cells travel in the blood stream, the surgical removal of a lump will not cure the cancer but just remove it from that one site.

Tumors may be removed from the brain if they are solitary, easily accessible, or not suitable for radiation. Although this may ease the symptoms, the long-term outlook is not good.

Treatment of fluid accumulation

Recurrent breast cancer can cause excessive fluid to accumulate around the lungs (pleural effusion) due to blockage of normal lymphatic drainage. This can cause shortness of breath or a sharp chest pain that worsens when taking a deep breath. Physical examination and a chest x-ray will diagnose it. It is usually treated with a 'chest tube' to drain the fluid. Once the fluid is gone, a drug (often doxycycline or bleomycin) or talcum powder is put into the pleural space to close it and prevent the fluid from reaccumulating.

Fluid may also accumulate in the abdomen and cause an uncomfortable swelling of the belly. A physician can usually make the diagnosis with a physical examination and confirm it with an ultrasound. If the fluid causes discomfort, temporary relief can be obtained if a catheter is inserted into the abdomen to drain the fluid. However, the fluid usually reaccumulates very quickly unless some other treatment of the cancer is given, such as chemotherapy or hormone treatment.

What can I do for myself?

Nutrition

Good nutrition is very important in maintaining a sense of well-being, but no studies show that diet alone can treat metastatic cancer. For many women with a recurrence, eating becomes difficult because they are fatigued or nauseated. In this situation, consultation with a nutritionist is important to learn ways to maintain an adequate diet. Chapter 35 discusses some of these issues.

Pain management

Pain may be present during recurrent breast cancer. Although radiation and systemic therapy may provide some relief, the use of regular and adequate medication is important to avoid letting the pain build up. It is important for you to find a drug that you tolerate well. With a physician's guidance you can increase the dose until the pain is relieved.

Many patients are uneasy about taking medications for pain, particularly if they are worried that the pills may be addictive or if they feel that taking medication for pain is a sign of 'giving in.' These thoughts are common. Most people will not become addicted to medications that are given to treat pain, and since being pain-free is essential for a good quality of life, it is not a 'weakness' or a sign of 'giving in' to treat the pain. It is simply allowing you to continue as many activities as possible for as long as possible. Unfortunately, all 'pain killers' have side effects, and narcotic medications most commonly cause severe constipation. This can be avoided by taking stool softeners and adequate dietary fiber and fluids as soon as the narcotic medication is started.

Mental well-being

Psychological well-being is also a very important part of the treatment of recurrent disease. Although the support of friends and family is crucial, individual counselling or discussion with a group of women with recurrent cancer may provide another means of support. Relaxation groups, massage therapy or other types of therapy may also help you cope with a new and frightening situation (see Chapter 36).

Palliative care

Palliative care concentrates on relieving the symptoms caused by the cancer rather than treating the cancer itself. Many centers have specialized palliative care teams that provide in-hospital and home care. These teams work cooperatively with the patient and her family to maintain an optimal quality of life. One of the goals is to allow the woman independence, dignity and choices during the difficult final phase of her life. Particular attention is paid to pain relief, nutrition, bowel care, psychological support and family needs.

SECTION FIFTEEN

Special Topics

CHAPTER FORTY

Breast cancer and pregnancy

THIS CHAPTER ANSWERS three questions:

1. What are my options if I receive a diagnosis of breast cancer while I am pregnant?

2. Does treatment of breast cancer affect my fertility?

3. Can I become pregnant after I have completed treatment for breast cancer?

If breast cancer is diagnosed during pregnancy

The procedure for diagnosing breast cancer is generally the same in the pregnant and the nonpregnant woman. Of course, care is taken to protect the fetus during chest x-rays by providing appropriate shielding. Also, bone scans should not be done since some of the radioactive particles may get into the fetus.

Deciding on a treatment plan

Treatment of breast cancer during pregnancy must be individualized: the woman and her family must be intimately involved in the decision-making. There are a number of factors to consider, including the stage of the cancer, the type of treatment required, and the gestational age of the fetus. In general, surgical therapy (mastectomy and axillary dissection) is safe and can proceed. Termination of pregnancy may be considered, not for a therapeutic effect but to allow treatment with chemotherapy and/or radiation if they are required. This is because chemotherapy and radiation can have a harmful effect on the fetus, particularly in the first trimester. In some circumstances mastectomy is appropriate, with adjuvant treatment delayed until after the birth. Occasionally, if the cancer is progressing very rapidly, a small risk of harm to the fetus may be accepted and chemotherapy or radiotherapy may be started, even while the fetus is still growing.

An obstetric evaluation should be done to determine the exact age of the fetus to help decide on the best time to deliver the baby. If an early delivery is an option, it should proceed before the breast cancer treatment starts. A delay in treatment of about four weeks is generally unlikely to affect the mother's chances of being cured, and will allow the baby to mature and have a better chance of being born healthy. The goal of any treatment is to achieve a good result for both the mother and the child. Each woman's situation is different, and requires careful consideration of all these options and in-depth discussion between the patient, her family, obstetrician, oncologist and surgeon to arrive at the best treatment plan.

Myths to dispel about breast cancer and pregnancy

Breast cancer is *not* more aggressive and does not have a worse outcome when it is discovered during pregnancy. Breast cancer does *not* spread to the fetus. Also, abortion of the fetus does not improve the outcome or have an effect on the growth of the mother's cancer.

Is fertility affected by breast cancer treatment?

Premenopausal women who receive chemotherapy may have their menstrual periods stop permanently and they may become infertile. This is more likely to occur as a woman gets older and nears the time of her normal menopause. For example, approximately 30% of women younger than 40 years but nearly all women older than 45 years will enter menopause after six months of chemotherapy. Sometimes menses return six months to a year after the chemotherapy is completed. However, since many women do remain fertile while receiving chemotherapy it is important to use effective methods of contraception (but not birth control pills) if you are sexually active. Radiation, unless it is directed at the pelvis, will not affect fertility.

Even if your menstrual periods are unaffected by chemotherapy, it is recommended that you do not get pregnant until six months after completing the treatment. Any residual effects of scattered radiation to the ovaries should also have resolved by six months. Tamoxifen (hormone therapy) is usually taken for longer periods of time and it is advised that you do not become pregnant while taking this drug.

Pregnancy after breast cancer

Women who get pregnant after having breast cancer have the same long-term outcome as women who have had breast cancer who do not become pregnant. There is no evidence that getting pregnant makes the cancer regrow or spread any more frequently or faster than if the woman does not get pregnant. There is also no increased chance of fetal malformations among babies born to women who have had breast cancer or treatment for breast cancer in the past.

Following radiation therapy of the breast, the normal breast tissue is altered. The normal engorgement in preparation for lactation does not occur, and during lactation very little, if any, milk is produced from the irradiated breast. However, breastfeeding from the unaffected breast is still possible and is encouraged.

Making the decision about whether to become pregnant

Apart from the biological considerations, a woman and her partner need to consider various social, psychological and economic implications of bearing a child. This is doubly hard when the mother-to-be is uncertain of her future. Often, delaying pregnancy for at least six months or more after the treatment is completed is a good idea, as it allows the woman's body and mind time to heal. Beyond these considerations there is no medical reason to delay pregnancy beyond six months. However, some doctors recommend a delay of two to five years to have greater confidence that the cancer won't recur.

In the final analysis, the woman, together with her family, needs to weigh the various possibilities, including her risk of cancer recurrence, the desire to have a baby, and her ability to care for the child if cancer recurs. If the woman and her family are counselled well, she can be encouraged to become pregnant if she so wishes.

CHAPTER FORTY-ONE

Are my daughters at risk?

Do my daughters have a higher risk of breast cancer?

THIS IS A FREQUENTLY asked question. At the outset, it is important to say that most daughters will not get breast cancer. However, because your daughters are female this means that they live with at least the 'average' risk of any woman. We also know that breast cancer can be passed on in families (Chapter 4) so the question really becomes, 'How much higher than the normal risk do my daughters face?'

To evaluate your daughter's risk of developing breast cancer several points need to be considered:

- How old were you when you developed breast cancer?
- Did the cancer affect one or both breasts?
- How many of your close relatives have breast cancer?
- How old is your daughter?
- Does your daughter have any other risk factors?

Your age at diagnosis

As women get older, the chance of developing breast cancer increases. This is unrelated to any special inherited tendency (see Chapter 3). Therefore, if the mother develops breast cancer at an older age, for example 75, the daughter's risk is only minimally higher. But if the mother developed cancer when she was 40 years old, it is more likely that something 'genetic' contributed to the cause of the cancer, and the daughter has an approximately four to five times higher than normal risk (see Chapter 4).

Cancer of one or both breasts

If both breasts are affected, the chance of a genetic tendency towards breast cancer is higher. If breast cancer of both breasts develops in a woman younger than 50 years old, this indicates a very substantially higher risk (five to ten times) in her daughters and also in her sisters. There is also evidence that a strong family history of breast cancer on the father's side can be passed on to a daughter, even though the father does not get breast cancer himself.

Number of family members with breast cancer

If many close blood relatives develop breast cancer (or cancer of the ovary or a type of cancer called 'sarcoma'), it is more likely that some genetic error is being passed within the family. This increases the risk to the daughter of an affected woman.

What does 'higher than normal risk' mean in numbers?

It's easiest to illustrate this with an example. Let's say a 58-year-old postmenopausal woman develops breast cancer in one breast and wonders how high her 30-year-old daughter's risk might be. The only other relative with breast cancer was one of the mother's aunts. This family history increases the daughter's risk by about 2.5 times the average. From Table 1 (p. 19), a typical 30-year-old woman has a 1 in 6,000 risk of getting breast cancer each year (not lifetime risk). If the daughter does not have any other risk factors, her chances are now 2.5 in 6,000 or approximately 1 in 2,400 per year. Over the next 10 years her risk is approximately 1 in 240 or about 0.4%. This is still not a very great risk and is not a reason to undertake any special steps. The daughter should be aware of the risk, participate in a program of breast health, and begin screening by mammography about ten years before the age at which her mother developed breast cancer (in this case, an age at which she might be recommended to have screening anyway).

Families with a strong history of breast cancer

Approximately 5% to 10% of breast cancers may be due to a unique genetic mutation such as in the BRCA1 or BRCA2 gene that is passed from generation to generation by either the father or the mother (see p. 29). In these families, relatives in three or more generations are often affected. A daughter of a woman with breast cancer from such a family would have a 50% lifetime risk of developing breast cancer. Also, in these families, cancers tend to occur roughly five to ten years earlier with each generation. Members of some of these families also tend to get other cancers more frequently, including cancers of the ovary, colon, brain and connective tissues.

Genetic counselling can estimate individual risk

If there is a very strong family history (three or more cases of breast cancer in direct blood relatives, i.e. mother/daughter, aunt/niece, sister) an unaffected member of the family may be interested in genetic counselling to assess more accurately her individual risk of developing breast cancer. During the counselling process a detailed family history is obtained and individual risk can be estimated. Some university medical schools and children's or specialty maternity hospitals have departments of medical genetics where such counselling can be obtained.

Genetic testing of members in high-risk 'breast cancer families' may soon be possible. Before going for testing, however, it is important to consider the implications of either a positive or negative test, and what action you might take with such information. Before genetic testing is done, specific counselling should be provided about the limitations of genetic testing and how to use the test results.

CHAPTER FORTY-TWO

Male breast cancer

The statistics

MEN DO HAVE BREAST TISSUE and can develop breast cancer, although it is not common. Breast cancer in a man usually appears as a lump under the nipple. Since men are not aware of their risk, they often ignore a lump for months or even years. By then, the cancer may have extended into the skin of the breast, the muscles beneath it and/or the lymph nodes, similarly to a locally advanced (stage III) cancer in a woman (see Chapter 17).

The diagnostic evaluation of the lump should be the same as for a woman and includes the use of bilateral mammograms and biopsy. The chances of survival and of controlling the cancer parallel that of a woman of the same age and depend on the stage of disease at diagnosis. Approximately 85% of breast cancers in men are estrogen-receptor positive.

Treatment

Treatment involves achieving local control, usually by mastectomy and axillary dissection. Breast conservation is rarely an issue for men. Radiation is added if the margins of excision are close to or involve the cancer or if multiple lymph nodes are involved in the axilla. There have been no scientific studies of adjuvant systemic therapy in men because the number of men with breast cancer is so small. In general, however, the course of breast cancer in men is very similar to that in women. Today, many oncologists recommend adding tamoxifen and/or chemotherapy to the surgery using the same indications as have been described for a woman of the same age in Chapters 28 and 30.

CHAPTER FORTY-THREE

Non-traditional methods of treatment

What are non-traditional treatments?

'NON-TRADITIONAL METHODS of treatment' is a term for a large number of health therapies that also can be referred to as 'unproven' methods of cancer treatment or 'alternative cancer therapy.' These methods need not be seen as alternatives to standard therapy, and sometimes, if they're not potentially harmful, may be used alongside standard therapy. Many of these treatments 'work' from the point of view of keeping hope alive and giving a woman a sense of control over her life again.

'Unproven methods' is a catch-all phrase that includes a variety of therapies, from vitamins to diets, from relaxation and therapeutic touch to herbal remedies, from immune stimulants to metabolic therapies. It is not clear that all of these therapies should be lumped into one category, but for the purposes of this chapter it is useful to discuss their similarities.

It is estimated that between 10% and 60% of cancer patients participate in some form of alternative therapy. When vitamins, relaxation methods and visualization are included in this category the number is probably larger.

Why are non-traditional treatments described as 'unproven'?

Most non-traditional remedies are referred to as 'unproven' because they have not been subjected to rigorous scientific testing. Physicians depend on extensive experiments and studies to assess new therapies and evaluate their effectiveness. With unproven therapies there may be individual testimonials that the therapy was beneficial, but this is not very dependable information because the particular circumstances and results cannot be confirmed, nor have the remedies been tested in a larger group of people to see if the results can be produced in a consistent way. This is not to say that the treatments have no validity, but most physicians feel uncomfortable placing their faith in a particular remedy without any scientific facts to support its use. As well, without more information, it is impossible to know about potential side effects of such treatments — even herbal methods may have severe side effects. It must be acknowledged, however, that much healing occurs outside the realm of science.

Why do patients use non-traditional treatments?

Many women seek alternative therapy when they feel that their physicians predict only 'doom and gloom.' If the oncologist appears to have little to offer or if the standard methods are not very predictable, it is appealing to try something that seems hopeful and positive. As well, many of the practitioners of holistic approaches are very charismatic and optimistic. Who wouldn't seek the reassurance of a practitioner who gives hope rather than one who seems more negative?

Many women also adopt unproven methods because of the power they feel in choosing the treatment and in directing their own care. This is a very positive attitude that helps one's psychological health during the ordeal of cancer therapy. This assertiveness shouldn't be restricted to choosing methods of alternative therapy. Each patient should participate in the decisions regarding her conventional treatment: the type of surgery, radiation, chemotherapy and hormones.

Not only does the patient often feel powerless, but so do many friends and family members, often steering patients towards non-traditional treatments because they want to help. Other patients simply have a general mistrust of the conventional medical establishment.

Non-traditional treatment methods also seem less toxic and more natural, with claims of boosting an individual's own immune system to attack the cancer in a natural way. Many patients claim that holistic programs are gentler, less invasive and more individualized.

Types of alternative treatments

The most common alternative cancer therapies can be categorized into the following groups: metabolic therapies, herbal remedies, mega-vitamins, diet therapy, visual imagery and immune therapy. There are also a large number of treatments that cannot be described in detail here.

Metabolic therapies

The concept of metabolic therapies is that toxins in the body cause and promote cancer, and that certain agents will detoxify the body, including laetrile, iscador (made from mistletoe) and hydrazine. Laetrile was tested in a large study run by the National Cancer Institute in the USA which failed to show that it was beneficial. As well, there have been some laetrile-related deaths, possibly due to the cyanide which is an active ingredient. The other treatments, iscador and hydrazine, have not been studied so it is difficult to assess their risks or benefits.

Herbal remedies

Herbal remedies have been used by healers for hundreds of years. Some of these remedies have been found to contain active agents that have become modern medicines. These include chemotherapy drugs such as vincristine and vinblastine from the periwinkle plant. Others, however, are considered to have secret, curative properties which remain untested. Comfrey, taheebo tea and Essiac can be included in the latter group. Essiac, which is now sold under a variety of names such as 'Fluressence,' was used initially by a nurse in Ontario to treat cancer in the 1920s. A large number of testimonials claimed that it had curative properties. For years the tea was distributed through the Canadian Health Protection Branch until the product became commercially available. In the 1980s a company did a scientific study of Essiac, but the results have never been published and are not available. Herbal remedies may not be completely safe; comfrey can cause liver damage and other herbs may be contaminated by dangerous fungi.

Mega-vitamins

Many people support mega-vitamin use. Vitamins are necessary for many of the chemical reactions in the body. It is claimed that high doses of vitamins, particularly vitamin C, can kill cancer cells and heal tissues. Although the normal diet does contain adequate amounts of vitamins for usual activities, there may be some benefit from higher doses of some vitamins. Unfortunately, all vitamins can cause severe side effects if the doses are too high, so a vitamin program should be discussed with your doctor.

Diet

'You are what you eat' is a phrase we have all heard. With respect to cancer, diet has been suggested as a cause by some and as a treatment by others. Various diets have been proposed as therapies for cancer. These include macrobiotic diets, vegetarian diets, grape diets, the Mormon diet and many others. However, without there being a simple cause for cancer, it is difficult to imagine that a diet alone can cure all malignancies, although dietary changes may be helpful to promoting overall health (see Chapter 35).

Immune therapy

Many treatments can be included in this group. These all depend on the theory that cancer is due to an immune defect, so if the immune system can be strengthened, then the cancer can be controlled. Although some cancers do seem to be directly related to the immune system, others occur without any obvious connection to our immune system, which is a very complex and

---

Open discussion builds trust

Although many patients are hesitant to discuss their interest in unproven methods of cancer treatment, it is important that the physician be informed for the benefit of both the patient and the doctor.

In an open and trusting atmosphere with their doctor, women need to be given the opportunity to explore unproven treatments. It is also necessary for physicians to explore and learn about these therapies to be able to advise and support their patients. There may be some therapies that are proven effective in some cases, or which lead to new discoveries. Physicians can also learn that some of the appeal of these therapies is the hope and optimism that they provide. Conventional medicine can learn that promoting a positive attitude can help, even in the most trying situations.

Patients who opt for non-traditional treatments should not be hesitant to maintain contact with, or return to, their conventional doctors when the time seems right.

---

poorly understood part of our make-up. Researchers and immunologists are struggling to determine what role the immune system has in the treatment of various cancers. At this time, despite years of research, there are many unanswered questions, and although vaccines and medications to boost the immune system may have some validity, there is no single treatment that has been proven to work against breast cancer.

Visual imagery and other forms of 'mental energy'

The concept of visual imagery is that mental energy can be focused through visualization to destroy cancer cells or stop their growth. Relaxation groups and meditation rely on the premise that a healthy mental attitude can aid healing. As well, other methods such as therapeutic touch, massage therapy and other physical techniques rely on the concept of the connection between mental attitude and physical health. While these therapies have not been proven to act on their own, they promote one's sense of responsibility and control in a way that can act with other healing remedies. The field of neuroendocrinology explores the connection between stress, health and the immune system and may lead to some important discoveries and treatments.

What are the risks of these treatments?

The risks of unproven therapies are related to the lack of scientific testing. We depend on regulations to keep our food safe. We test and categorize which additives are approved, and legally require that they be listed on the box or package to protect us as consumers. We have none of these safeguards with unproven cancer treatments. As well, the costs can be prohibitive. A therapy that promises a 'cure' makes people with cancer susceptible to paying potentially large amounts of money regardless of the lack of firm evidence of benefit.

The practitioners of non-traditional methods may be very ethical and well-meaning, but there are no safeguards to protect patients from quacks and crooks that are also in the business. It is important that patients who seek alternative therapies be directed to people with a reputation for honesty and reasonable cost.

Another problem is that if the cancer does not respond to a change in, say, behavior or diet, the patient then feels like a failure. Many people already (mistakenly) feel totally responsible for getting cancer in the first place — due to their diet, or stress in their past. Although accepting responsibility for making treatment choices is worthwhile, blaming oneself can be very damaging.

Finally, some cancers are very treatable and can be cured with standard therapy. Although every patient should have a choice of treatment, there are concerns that when curative treatment is rejected in favor of unproven methods, the chance of being cured may be lost because of a delay in initiating the proper anti-cancer treatment.

Clinical research:
Looking for better answers

Why are clinical studies important?

As MOST WOMEN quickly learn, there are a lot of unanswered questions about breast cancer (and many other diseases). What is/are the cause(s)? Can we prevent it? What new treatment or approach might give better results than we're getting right now? Is there some way of curing breast cancer permanently?

Research studies (also called 'trials') are set up to try to answer these and other questions. It's an ongoing process, with questions constantly being asked, and researchers constantly looking for better ways of treating patients in every area of medicine. Sometimes we even forget that the treatments we're using now for breast cancer (drugs, surgery, radiation) were at one time part of a study in which a group of researchers were trying something new.

What are the steps in testing a new treatment?

All potential treatments go through the same type of rigorous evaluation process that can be illustrated with the example of the testing of a new drug.

All new drug treatments begin in the laboratory. If extensive tests in test tubes and mice show that a new drug has potential in treating breast cancer, then it is tested in humans in a preliminary (phase 1) study to check on side effects and to establish a dose for which the side effects are acceptable. Then, the drug is tested in a small group of women to determine its effect in controlling the cancer (phase 2). At this stage the question is, 'Does the drug work at a dose that is safe in humans?' Phase 1 and 2 studies usually involve women with advanced or metastatic breast cancer.

If the results are still promising, the question then arises whether the new drug is better than the 'standard' treatment. To determine this, a third (phase 3) study is done in which women are randomly selected for either the new or old treatment. If it is not known which treatment is superior, it is ethical to compare the treatments in consenting, volunteer women.

Scientific studies such as these must follow rigid statistical rules to confirm that the information gained is reliable and repeatable. It is also important to realize that patients must give their consent before they are included in any study.

What should I do if I'm asked to be part of a study?

Participation in any study is strictly voluntary. It is important for any patient enrolling in a study to understand why it is being set up, what is already known of the treatment's side effects and benefits and what the alternatives are. Many phase 2 and 3 trials use drugs that have been studied already, so there may be considerable information available on the treatment. On the other hand, it is important to understand that the primary aim of a phase 1 trial is to define the side effects.

Before any study is done, hospital ethics committees evaluate each study to ensure that the rights of the patients are protected and that the study is ethical in its design and implementation. These ethics committees always include members of the lay public. An informed consent must be obtained from each patient before enrolment in the study. The researcher must carefully discuss the study with each potential participant, explaining the reasons for it, the risks and benefits, and other options the patient has in terms of treatment. The patient should not sign unless she has had all her questions answered thoroughly.

Ultimately, each woman must feel free to decide what is in her best interests, and must be comfortable in choosing to be a part of a study. Also, she must understand that her standard of care will not change if she subsequently decides to withdraw from it. It is through the commitment of thousands of women participating in clinical research that many advances have been made in the treatment of breast cancer.

CHAPTER FORTY-FIVE

Women's awareness and advocacy

by Judith Caldwell

I am only one; but still I am one. I cannot do everything; but I can still do something. I will not refuse to do something I can do.

— *Helen Keller*

WHEN I WAS IN HIGH SCHOOL my friend Cathy's mother developed breast cancer. We whispered about 'it' behind Cathy's back, never asking her how everything was at home. We weren't heartless, only frightened, embarrassed and unable to find the right words. Unconsciously we may have thought that if we denied that one of our favorite moms was stalked by a disease no one ever spoke of, it would go away and leave us unscathed.

Thirty-five years later, with three years of survival under my belt, I know that silence kills, denial kills, and that as an advocate, my job is to break the silence and shine an uncompromising light on all the issues surrounding breast cancer.

We each experience breast cancer differently. Yet, most of us ride a roller coaster of overwhelming anxiety, grief, sadness, anger, frustration, love of life, black humor...and the fear of a truncated future. On our bodies there is an indelible physical reminder, however small, that our lives have been put in peril —

that breast cancer pursues us. Advocacy offers a means to channel our energies and to do something positive about a situation which we could not prevent and over which we had no control. It is a way to save other lives.

Most of us who develop breast cancer are taken by surprise, with no family history or obvious high risk factors. We face an instant crash course just learning enough about the disease to make critical treatment choices. Usually it is not until the immediate crisis of diagnosis and treatment decisions has passed that an awareness emerges of the staggering scope of breast cancer among women in general. A 'Why me?' cry changes to 'Why *not* me?' when the huge numbers of women affected becomes apparent. In North America tens of thousands of women die prematurely from breast cancer every year, and approximately two million women are living with a previous diagnosis of the disease.

Why has breast cancer become such a hot, public topic? Is it because of our aging population, with more women edging into the most susceptible age brackets? Is it because sexual issues are more in the open? Is it because breast cancer advocacy groups have finally emerged, demanding decent funding for research?

As advocates it is our job to let other women know the realities of breast cancer and to encourage them to take care of themselves. Across the country, information is not equally available to every cultural and language group. Not all women understand how to perform breast self-examination. Nor are they aware that the earlier the diagnosis, the better the options will be. Not all women are taking advantage of screening mammography programs that can detect tumors two to five years before they can be felt. Not all women realize that their doctors are here to serve them, and that they have rights to full information, second opinions and treatment choices.

With this disease we also have to confront the uncomfortable issue of breasts and the values of femininity, sexuality and nurturing we have placed upon them. We relish memories of babies nursing at our breasts, a lover's caress and those we cherish being held in a soft embrace. On every newsstand, in every movie and TV show, we are swamped with images exploiting cleavage and creating expectations of how a woman must look to be womanly.

The public must come to know that breast cancer treatment is about saving lives and that even with changed bodies, life, love, sex and femininity carry on. A re-evaluation of priorities and values in the shadow of breast cancer may yield a more conscious appreciation of life.

The tools of advocacy are information, facts, figures and a clear understanding of the social and financial impact of the disease. However, these things are not enough! The 'personal' is 'political' and stories of women and families facing breast cancer must be told. The pain of lost battles must be heard and the hope that comes from long-time survivors spread. Decisions are influenced by gut reactions as well as logic. At the current funding levels only a few researchers can afford to turn their attention to breast cancer. We need to attract more money and to convince our governments and corporations to set priorities.

So, what can one person do?

- **Educate yourself.** Learn as much as you can about the disease and the issues surrounding it.
- **Find others.** Place an ad in the local newspaper asking for others interested in the issue to contact you. Host a meeting.
- **Focus.** Advocacy comes in many forms — support groups, fundraising, education or political lobbying. Be bold in asking people with the skills you need to work with you.
- **Network.** Join other breast cancer groups locally, nationally and internationally.
- **Speak out** courageously in public.

I know in my bones that even one person speaking out can have an impact. Two people determined to bring breast cancer issues forward can move small mountains, and a group of people passionate about making a difference can mobilize an entire community, indeed an entire country.

Each of us is only one, but we can still do something.

Glossary

Adjuvant therapy Treatment that is given in addition to the initial surgery (that removes all visible evidence of breast cancer) to help prevent the cancer from recurring. Often called 'insurance' against recurrence of cancer.

Androgen Male hormone that may be used as a drug to treat breast cancer.

Atypical cells Cells that appear abnormal but not cancerous when viewed under the microscope.

Axilla The underarm area between the armpit and the collarbone.

Benign tumor A tumor that is not cancerous.

Biopsy The surgical procedure in which a small piece of tissue is removed to be studied under the microscope to help make a diagnosis.

Breast implant A round or tear drop-shaped sac filled with salt water that is placed under the skin and muscle of the chest wall after mastectomy to recreate a breast shape or improve the shape of an existing breast.

Breast prosthesis An artificial breast form that can be worn externally to replace the breast shape after a mastectomy.

Breast reconstruction Surgical procedures (several types) that recreate a breast shape or nipple after a mastectomy. This may involve insertion of a breast implant or creation of a breast shape from other body tissues.

Calcifications Tiny deposits of calcium that may signify cancer and can be seen on a mammogram.

Carcinoma Another word for cancer.

Cancer The abnormal and uncontrolled growth of cells that may invade and destroy surrounding tissues.

Chemotherapy Treatment for cancer involving the use of drugs.

Clinical trial A carefully designed scientific experiment for testing a new therapy or treatment approach.

Cyst A non-cancerous sac filled with fluid.

Dissection Surgical cutting open of any part of the body.

Edema Swelling of body tissue due to accumulation of fluid. May occur in the arm or breast after removal of lymph nodes during treatment for breast cancer.

Estrogen A sex hormone that is responsible for the development of female characteristics such as breasts and broadening of hips. It also has a key role in the menstrual cycle and pregnancy and stimulates the growth of some breast cancers.

Estrogen receptor A protein in the cancer cell that binds to the hormone estrogen. A cancer cell that is estrogen receptor-rich (or positive) is usually sensitive to hormones.

Fine needle aspiration A biopsy technique in which a thin needle is inserted into the body and a few cells or some fluid is removed for diagnosis.

Fine wire localization A technique to direct a surgical biopsy to an area of the breast which is abnormal on a mammogram but which cannot be felt. A thin wire is placed into the breast under mammographic control to guide the surgeon to the correct part of the breast to be removed.

Hormone therapy Treatment for breast cancer that involves altering the hormone levels in the body. This may involve removing the ovaries or the use of specific drugs.

Hormones Chemicals produced by specific parts of the body (glands) that travel through the blood stream to another location in the body where they cause a change in a structure or function (e.g. estrogen in young women is produced in the ovaries and causes the breasts to develop).

Hyperplasia Cells that divide and accumulate in excessive numbers but are not yet cancerous.

In situ breast cancer Cancer growing within the milk ducts or milk glands of the breast.

Invasive cancer Cancer that has spread from its original location into adjacent tissues or organs.

Lobules (lobular) The milk glands in the breast.

Lumpectomy A surgical procedure in which the tumor and a small margin of surrounding normal breast tissue is removed. Other terms include partial mastectomy, segmental mastectomy, wide excision and breast conservation.

Lymph nodes Small lima bean-shaped structures grouped at various locations along the lymph system in the body (e.g. armpits, neck, groin). They act as the main 'filters' to defend against infections and may be a location to where cancer spreads. Lymph nodes under the arm are frequently removed as part of breast cancer surgery.

Lymphatic system The network of vessels throughout the body that carries lymph fluid to and from all the tissues of the body. Its main function is to fight off infection.

Lymphedema *See* **Edema.**

Malignant tumor A tumor that is harmful because it grows out of control and invades and destroys surrounding tissues.

Mammogram An x-ray of the breast.

Mastectomy The surgical procedure in which the whole breast is removed. Partial mastectomy See Lumpectomy.

Menopause The time of life when a woman's monthly periods stop because her ovaries have stopped making estrogen.

Metastasis The spread of a cancer from one part of the body to another.

Microcalcifications Very tiny calcifications.

Necrosis The death of cells in some part of the body's tissue.

Oncologist A doctor who specializes in the treatment of cancer.

Palpation Examination with the hands; to feel.

Pathologist A doctor who specializes in the structure and function of cells and tissues of the body, and who studies how the various changes relate to specific diseases.

Primary cancer The cancer in the original location where it was first detected.

Progesterone A female sex hormone involved in a number of functions, including the menstrual cycle and pregnancy.

Prognosis An estimate of the expected course of the disease.

Prophylactic A preventive treatment which can involve any type of therapy, e.g. drugs, surgery, radiation.

Prosthesis An artificial device that is attached to the body to substitute for a part of the body that is missing.

Radiotherapy (radiation therapy) The use of high-energy x-rays for the treatment of cancer.

Recurrence The reappearance of cancer following a period of time when there was no evidence of disease. The recurrence may be either at the original site (a local recurrence), in the adjacent lymph nodes (a regional recurrence) or elsewhere in the body (a systemic or distant recurrence).

Risk factor Something that increases your chances of getting a disease, either acquired from the environment, or inherited.

Sarcoma A type of cancer arising from the connecting tissues (muscles, bones, nerves, etc).

Screening Tests done on a person who is feeling well, with no symptoms, to detect evidence of unsuspected disease.

Secondary cancer A cancer that has spread to another site. Also called 'metastatic cancer.'

Staging A procedure involving a variety of tests to establish the extent of the cancer at the time of diagnosis.

Subcutaneous The area underneath the skin.

Sutures Stitches used to close up a surgical wound.

Systemic Affecting the body in general rather than one specific part.

Tamoxifen A drug widely used to treat breast cancer metastases and help prevent the recurrence of breast cancer. It is an anti-estrogen drug since its main action is to block the growth-stimulating effects of estrogen on cancer cells. It is a common form of 'hormone therapy.'

Tumor Abnormal growth of tissue. Can be cancerous (malignant) or noncancerous (benign).

White blood cells Cells in the blood stream that detect and fight infection, 'foreign' material and abnormal cells.

Additional Reading

Healthy Eating

Jane Brody's Good Food Gourmet. Jane E. Brody. Bantam Books. New York, 1992.
Lighthearted Everyday Cooking. Anne Lindsay. Macmillan of Canada. Toronto, 1991.
Rose Reisman Brings Home Light Cooking. Rose Reisman. Macmillan of Canada. Toronto, 1993.
The Lighthearted Cookbook. Anne Lindsay. Key Porter Books. Toronto, 1988.
The Nutrition Challenge for Women. Louise Lambert-Lagace. Stoddart Publishing. Toronto, 1989.

Coping/Relaxation

Books

Affirmations, Meditations and Encouragements for Women Living with Breast Cancer. Linda Dackman. Harper Collins. New York, 1993.
Cancervive. Susan Nessin and Joyce Ellis. Houghton Mifflin Co. Boston, 1991.
Getting Well Again. Stephanie Matthews-Simonton, O. Carl Simonton, James L. Creighton. Bantam Books. New York, 1978.

273

Living Beyond Limits: New Hope and Help for Facing Life-Threatening Cancer. David Spiegel. Times Books. New York, 1993.
Love is Letting Go of Fear. Gerald Jampolsky. Celestial Arts. Berkeley, 1979.
Love, Medicine and Miracles. Bernie Siegel. Harper & Row. New York, 1986.
Minding the Body, Mending the Mind. Joan Borysenko. Bantam Books. New York, 1988.
Spinning Straw into Gold. Ronnie Kaye. Simon and Shuster. New York, 1991.
The Relaxation Response. Herbert Benson and Miriam Z. Klipper. Avon Books. New York, 1976.

Audiotapes
(Often available where health books are sold.)
Cancer and The Whole Person. Lee Pulos.
Letting Go of Stress. Emett Miller.
Series of Time In Tapes. Lis Smith. (available for $10.00 & postage) from B.C. Cancer Agency, Patient and Family Counselling Services, 600 W. 10th Ave., Vancouver, B.C. Canada v5z 4E6
The Healing Journey. Emett Miller.

Personal Stories

My Breast. Joyce Wadler. Pocket Books. New York, 1992.
Picasso's Woman. Rosalind McPhie. Douglas and McIntyre. Toronto, 1994.
That Other Place. Penelope Williams. Dundurn. Toronto, 1993.

Talking to Children

Afraid to Ask: A Book about Cancer. Judylaine Fine. Kids Can Press. Toronto, 1984.
Helping Children Understand: A Guide for a Parent with Cancer. (booklet) American Cancer Society. Minnesota, 1986.

General Information

Dr. Susan Love's Breast Book. Susan Love and Karen Lindsey. Addison Wesley. New York, 1991.

More Detailed Medical Information

Diseases of the Breast (textbook). Edited by Harris J., Lippman M., Morrow M., Hellman S. Lippincott-Raven. Philadelphia, 1996.

On Internet

Access an open discussion forum about Breast Cancer by sending a message to: listserver@morgan.usc.mun.ca   with text "subscribe breast-cancer (your name)".

Intelligent Patient Guide maintains a web site for information related to this publication. The address is: http://www.ipguide.com

Index